Volume XXIX: NUMBER TWO
2004

Contents

Modern Psychoanalysis

EDITOR Phyllis W. Meadow

MANAGING EDITOR Ronald Okuaki Lieber

EDITORIAL BOARD

Arnold Bernstein Jane G. Goldberg
June Bernstein Robert J. Marshall
Mimi G. Crowell Leslie Rosenthal
George Ernsberger Muriel Sackler
Martin Gliserman Sara Sheftel

BOOK REVIEWS Elizabeth Dorsey Steven Poser

BOARD OF CONSULTANTS

Peter L. Giovacchini Louis R. Ormont
Marvin Koven Murray H. Sherman
Leonard Liegner Hyman Spotnitz

EDITORIAL ASSISTANT Linda S. Rode

The Editors invite submissions of articles to MODERN PSYCHOANALYSIS. Manuscripts should be typed, double-spaced, on one side of 8½ × 11 inch white paper, or on a 3½ inch disk. The first page should start halfway down from the top, and should be submitted in triplicate with a SASE. Footnotes and bibliographies must conform to the style of this journal. The Editors should be informed, with the submission, if the article has appeared or has been submitted elsewhere.

MODERN PSYCHOANALYSIS, the journal of the Center for Modern Psychoanalytic Studies, 16 West 10th Street, New York, NY 10011, is published semiannually. Individual subscriptions are on a yearly basis: $53.00 per year. Institutions: $60.00. Write for foreign rates.

ISBN 0-9764359-4-2 YBK Publishers, Inc., 425 Broome St., New York, NY 10013

MODERN PSYCHOANALYSIS is abstracted and indexed in *Psychoanalytic Abstracts* (Pa. A). Copyright © 2004 by the Center for Modern Psychoanalytic Studies. ISSN: 0361-5227

Single-Case-Study Methodology and the Contact Function

MARY SHEPHERD

Modern analysts have spent over three decades refining a methodology for single-case-study research that is both appropriate for psychoanalysis and acceptable to the canons of scientific inquiry. This paper suggests that the modern psychoanalytic concept of the contact function is an important contribution to this work. The contact function is a window on the unconscious functioning of the patient in the transference and can therefore be used to ensure that the universe of observation is non-reactive. It also functions as an indicator of closeness or distance to the analyst and so can provide a check on the findings.

The always beleaguered single-case study remains the royal road to knowledge in psychoanalysis. Only in this context can the researcher gain direct access to unconscious processes, access which is experienced as well as observed. As soon as analyst and patient begin meeting at an agreed-upon time for an agreed-upon fee, patterns begin to emerge that reveal the unconscious functioning of both parties within a controlled environment. Only within the context of the analytic contract can knowledge of unconscious processes be studied in a systematic way. For better or worse psychoanalysis is about transference. Transference is the strange thing that happens once a contract is agreed on and that continues to reveal that something is happening that is somehow different from what appears to be happening. Transference is the evidence of unconscious processes. Though it exists as a phenomenon everywhere—in couples, families, schools, and groups of all kinds—and though its manifestations can be observed and inferences made in quasi-controlled situations, only within

© 2004 CMPS/*Modern Psychoanalysis*, Vol. 29, No. 2

the psychoanalytic contract can it be studied directly in a controlled way. "If . . . the process takes place outside of the treatment situation, only those parts of a theory can be tested that do not need a special interpersonal relation as a basis"(Thoma & Kachele, 1975 qtd. in Wallerstein, 1988, p. 19). The fact that this complex phenomenon persists in this environment in spite of suggestion, advice, common sense, insight, interpretation, goodwill, and any other instrument of influence brought to bear on it leaves us with a force to be reckoned with, wrestled with, studied, understood, and uncovered. The fact that the transference is the avenue to both knowledge and cure creates the immense problems and opportunities that a field over a hundred years old is still grappling with. The problems of replication and of the participant-observer-clinician-scientist will not go away.

The challenge to Freud's energy concepts brought to a head by the hermeneutical theorists in the '70s and '80s (Spence, 1982; Holt, 1981) was compelling enough to convince a large number of American analysts to abandon the claim that psychoanalysis is a natural science making verifiable claims about the nature of mental functioning. They became content to leave the psychoses to medicine (Shepherd, 1999) and concentrate on narrative coherence (Ricoeur, 1977) as a measure of psychoanalytic success. The clinician is not a researcher/scientist but rather a seeker of subjective truth with the patient. Interpretive "fit" replaces veridical explanation. Replication is no longer important if the search for general laws is abandoned. "It [narrative truth] is first and foremost highly relative; each story is different and what makes a particular formulation persuasive and compelling is precisely the fact that it is carefully tailored to the patient's life . . . but if each piece of narrative truth is relative, how can we build it into a general theory?" (Spence, 1982, p. 63) Although this movement provided a much needed corrective to the faltering tenability of reconstruction as psychoanalytic goal and introduced a refreshing emphasis on the centrality of the present, its insistence that there are no discoverable "causes" for the phenomena in analysis, no quantities of stimulation, no organism struggling to get its primal needs met, no unconscious conundrums left psychoanalysis to founder in a sea of subjectivity. It might be accurate to say that the hermeneutical movement would make psychoanalysis a discipline of consciousness.

Modern Psychoanalysis and the Single-Case Study

Fortunately for psychoanalysis modern analysts have spent the last three decades writing, refining, thinking, and rethinking the problems of single-case-study research and the status of psychoanalysis as a natural science. Because of their work with the psychoses, modern analysts were loath to relinquish the energy concepts which had such explanatory power for the phenomena they were encountering. Their clinical papers constitute a rich contribution to the understanding and treatment of narcissism. Simultaneously they refined the methodological guidelines for formal single-case research. This combination of work created a "culture of research" (Emde & Fonagy, 1997) in New York and Boston (Bernstein, 1992; McAloon, 1992; Soldz & McCullough, 1999; Crowell, 1992; Sheftel, 1992; Lief, 1992). As they trained analysts and prepared for the doctorate in psychoanalysis, they have made significant contributions to single-case research methodology. As Meadow (1992) states the challenge, "The major problem for psychoanalysis, if it intends to qualify as a reputable science, lies in its ability to develop its own method for observing events" (p. 137).To that end much progress has been made. Over 215 research papers have been written following dissertation guidelines. Advanced candidates are required to undertake a formal research project in order to obtain their certification. The purpose is to "further develop the candidate's ability to comprehend and utilize patient's communications. . . . [Students] . . . further refine their ability to integrate concept with observation. They learn the art of listening, measuring, and classifying raw data to give meaning to what is observable" (Meadow, 1984, p. 124). The candidates develop a question about their case, state the assumptions, review the literature, and then proceed to collect and classify data according to conditions established before the data collection begins.

The most important contribution modern psychoanalysis has made to this process is the idea, articulated and developed by Meadow in papers from 1984 through 1995, that psychoanalysis is a "natural experiment." As patient and analyst meet together over time for an agreed-upon fee, the events that occur repetitively within the dyad are similar to naturally occurring events in any other controlled domain. The analyst is like an anthropologist in a walled village, studying a universe as it unfolds before him or her over time. The element of repetition of the dyadic events makes it possible to conduct either qualitative or quantitative studies within this universe. "The greatest strength of the psychoanalytic research method is its ability to investigate, in detail, particular aspects of human nature without separating them from the entirety of the personality" (Meadow, 1984, p. 126). As opposed to an experiment with manipulated variables, this "natural experiment" allows the researcher/analyst to study the functioning of the patient as he/she relates to the analyst in a myriad of repetitive ways over time. If theory confirmation or disconfirmation is the goal, the analyst may set up a study that predicts ways in which various aspects of the patient's personality will interact with each other or if she/he hopes to generate new hypotheses, he/she may choose to study a symptom, fantasy, defense, or particular production as it shifts in relation to other parts of the personality. In any case, central to the research is the operationalizing of concepts. The researcher must state clearly what his data will "look like." He must also pre-establish the parameters of the study. "The entire predictive complex of conditions . . . is set down *in advance*" (Wallerstein, 1964, p. 684). This protects against post hoc explanations and theorizing and provides a context for falsifiability. Though each case reveals general laws of psychic functioning, each patient represents a unique patterning of instinctual forces and therefore constitutes a potential wealth of new knowledge. Uniqueness within repetition is the analyst's data field. While the study cannot obviously be duplicated by another researcher, the findings can be checked with future events in the analysis. This approach to research addresses the replication problem. As students and, later, analysts learn to operationalize their concepts, classify them, and set up the conditions for answering their question in the repetitive natural universe of an analysis, basic conditions for research are met.

The second hurdle for psychoanalytic research, the analyst/researcher as participant-observer is surmounted to some extent by the fact that an analyst, by definition, has spent years in training to be able to use him/herself as an experiencing but unbiased observer. The personal analysis, self-analysis, supervisory analysis, and research supervision provide a continual check on the observations of the analyst/researcher. While far from perfect, this is a much more rigorous monitor of validity than that in any social science participant-observer method, which tends to rely on conscious self-awareness to control for bias. These analytic controls, coupled with the methods mentioned above, provide a powerful means for crosschecking. The operationalized concepts, described in advance, together with predictive hypotheses or hypothesis-generating material, combine to control for analytic bias.

A third consideration has arisen as these methods have been refined and perfected by successive analytic graduates. By 1995, Meadow emphasized that

> in our use of the single case study we should be clear, both to ourselves and to philosophers of science, that we are not engaging in clinical research, even though we are using clinical observations as the field of our investigations. This cannot be overemphasized. The object of our

investigations is the functioning human psyche, not the effectiveness of interventions or outcomes of treatment. In this approach to research, it is important to bear in mind that the accuracy of explanations cannot be confirmed by a patient's acceptance of an explanation. (p. 26)

She goes on to say, "prediction of outcomes cannot be central to depth research; prediction of mental and emotional tendencies can." As students perfected their methods, their studies improved and many approached the ideal of isolating psychic functions, studying their interaction, and offering in-depth explanations. In some cases, however, it began to seem as though this emphasis on operationalized concepts was leading the student away from the unconscious dynamics of the patient in the transference. One patient, in an excellent study, was clearly regressing in a reactive way to the interventions the analyst was making. This was a patient who would undoubtedly have regressed under the best of circumstances, but because the interventions and their effect were not included in the study (there was no methodological vehicle in place to consider this problem and factor it out), it was not possible to evaluate what within the patient's own "mind" triggered the regression. Only when the patient is relatively free from reactive behavior can the analyst proceed to study his mental functioning.

So it appears that good research and good therapy are good bedfellows. Meadow insists that good research go beyond the circular thinking of the "tally argument" [Freud's contention that an interpretation is true if the patient accepts it as real for himself (Bucci, 1989)] and provide methods that allow for the discovery of new explanatory concepts. It also follows that good treatment is a sine qua non for good research. The analyst needs to be operating in such a way as to allow the "natural experiment" to unfold freely. Similarly, even though the researcher is not studying the effectiveness of interventions, his/her interventions need to be adequate enough to not trigger a reactive regression. The problem of countertransference resistance can interfere with both these goals. It is always difficult since the person in its grip, of course, does not see it. So, in addition to supervision and self-analysis, is there any additional methodological tool that can help this problem?

Contact Function and Research

This question brings us back to the transference and to the relationship the patient wants to have with the analyst. The contact function, a concept developed by Spotnitz (2004), is the patient's "occasional verbal attempt to gratify an immediate need for words from the analyst" (p. 116). It represents the struggle of the early infant to control the mother. The way the analyst responds to the contact controls the resistance. Or, as stated by Meadow (1984), "the contact function replaces the subjectively determined timing of classical interpretation with what might be called 'demand feeding' in which the timing and type of communication are [determined by] what the subject asks for" (p. 92). This concept is central to the paradigm shift (Shepherd, 1999) accomplished by Spotnitz from the insight/interpretation model of psychoanalytic technique in which the interventions are driven more by the theoretical position of the analyst and cure is defined by self awareness, to the neuro-biological/maturation model wherein interventions are designed to resolve the patient's resistance to growth, and cure is defined by satisfying and healthy functioning, with insight a probable byproduct but not a vehicle for change. In this model the treatment is led by the needs of the patient. The patient leads the analyst by indicating the levels of frustration and gratification he can tolerate and keep talking productively. Too much gratification and the resistance is submerged; too much frustration and the patient regresses. Again, as Bernstein (1992) puts it, the contact function "represents a point where conscious interest and unconscious resistance converge" (p. 185). Margolis (1994) reviews the concept and explains how it not only serves to reveal the form that the patient's resistance takes from moment to moment, but also constitutes a constant measure of the degree of narcissism or relatedness the patient wants to establish in the treatment and is therefore a crucial measure of progress. The contact function is essentially the guide to the treatment of the patient, but it is also, in effect, a window on the transference, both in the moment and in the deeper layers of closeness or distance to the analyst. Consequently, to incorporate it into research methods can add an important dimension to both research and treatment.

Spotnitz (1992) warns about destructive research. He says that "the basic principle of analytic therapy is to provide enough gratification so patients do not regress into psychosis. Research interests do not supercede that fundamental tenet" (p. 135). A clearly defined study of the contact and the analyst's response to it included in single-case-study methodology could serve as a check or control on the analysis, as well as on the research. The researcher would have to take into account the "position" (closer or more distant), reactions (to his/her interventions), and state of being (affect or lack thereof) in his discussion and would thereby have an "objective" look at how the treatment is progressing. This would also clarify things for any colleague or supervisor assisting with the research and would enable her to correct problems as the research is going on. Any countertransference problems negatively affecting the patient could be corrected and the free flow of the "natural experiment" restored. Adding this ingredient to the methodological "team" would in no way limit the scope or subject of the study. It would simply be an additional factor to be included in the research. Whatever the findings, it would be necessary to discuss them in relation to this analysis of the contact. The researcher/analyst would be required *by the research* to take into account the contact and his response to it (the countertransference) as well as any aspect of the patient's productions he/she has chosen to study. This would assure him/her that the material he was studying was resistance-free. Thus the contact would be a control on the findings, and the findings may add valuable information to the management of the transference. The researcher may discover, for example, that certain conflicts, defenses, fantasies, or types of functioning are prevalent when the patient is distant and others prevail as the patient moves closer. This methodology allows psychoanalytic research to approach unconscious material from two directions. It is unique to and proper for psychoanalysis and constitutes a powerful tool for exploring deeper explanations of unconscious material.

REFERENCES

Bernstein, J. (1992), The research method in the making of a psychoanalyst. *Modern Psychoanalysis*, 17:203–229.

Bucci, W. (1989), Reconstruction of Freud's tally argument. *Psychoanalytic Inquiry*, 9:249–281.

Crowell, M. (1992), Supervising institute candidates in psychoanalytic case research. *Modern Psychoanalysis*, 17:197–202.

Emde, R. & P. Fonagy (1997), An emerging culture for psychoanalytic research. *International Journal of Psychoanalysis*, 78:224–228.

Holt, R. (1981), The death and transfiguration of metapsychology. *International Review of Psychoanalysis*, 8:129–143.

Lief, E. (1992), Preliminary guidelines for single-case research. *Modern Psychoanalysis*, 17:231–250.

Margolis, B. (1994), *Selected Papers on Modern Psychoanalysis. Modern Psychoanalysis*, 19.

McAloon, R. (1992), A historical survey of psychoanalytic research. *Modern Psychoanalysis*, 17:161–181.

Meadow, P. (1984), Issues in psychoanalytic research. *Modern Psychoanalysis*, 9:123–147.

—— (1992) Is psychoanalysis a science? *Modern Psychoanalysis*, 17:137–160.

—— (1995), Psychoanalysis: an open system of research. *Modern Psychoanalysis*, 20:3–30.

Ricoeur, P. (1977), The question of proof in Freud's psychoanalytic writings. *Journal of the American Psychoanalytic Association*, 25:835–871.

Sheftel, S. (1992), Relearning the research process: on the connection between research and treatment. *Modern Psychoanalysis*, 17:203–229.

Shepherd, M. (1999), The silent revolution in psychoanalysis: Hyman Spotnitz and the reversibility of schizophrenia. Unpublished paper. pp. 1–41.

Soldz, S. & L. McCullough, eds. (1999) *Reconciling Empirical Knowledge and Clinical Experience: The Art and Science of Psychotherapy.* Washington, DC: American Psychological Association.

Spence, D. (1982), Narrative truth and theoretical truth. *Psychoanalytic Quarterly*, 51:43–69.

Spotnitz, H. (1995) A note on psychoanalytic research. *Modern Psychoanalysis*, 17:133–136.

—— (2004), *Modern Psychoanalysis of the Schizophrenic Patient*. 2004 Second Edition. New York: YBK Publishers.

Wallerstein, R. (1964), The role of prediction in theory building in psychoanalysis. *Journal of the American Psychoanalytic Association*, 12:675–691.

—— (1988), Psychoanalysis, psychoanalytic science, and psychoanalytic research. *Journal of the American Psychoanalytic Association*, 36:3–30.

36 Hawthorn Street
Cambridge, MA 02138
maryshepherd@comcast.net

The Case Study in Psychoanalytic Education

NIGEL MACKAY
STEVEN POSER

The case study is widely used in psychoanalysis for presenting and illustrating clinical theory. It is also the standard means by which analysts-in-training demonstrate their ability both to manage cases and to convey their grasp of the case material. Most training institutes use the formal presentation of a case as a requirement for graduation. The Center for Modern Psychoanalytic Studies, New York, currently requires a single-case study as a final piece for the completion of certificate training (Meadow & Bernstein, 1999). In this paper we argue that the main purpose of the training case study is to illustrate theory systematically in clinical material and that treating the case study as an illustration addresses the main controversies over the legitimacy of the case study as a research method and, in particular, suits the needs of clinical training. In the light of this we set out a structure for the case study, giving its components and sequence and a rationale for this structure.

The case study is the standard means for presenting and illustrating clinical theory in psychoanalysis and is usually the means by which analysts-in-training demonstrate their ability both to manage cases and to convey their grasp of the case material. In what follows we set out a structure for the case study and discuss its components.

There are many ways of writing a case study. In some respects the case study is like a novel, and, like a good novel, much of the effect of a good case study derives from the author's narrative skill, the ability to convey the texture and drama of the human story that is unfold-

© 2004 CMPS/*Modern Psychoanalysis*, Vol. 29, No. 2

ing before the analyst. Good novels are only partially restricted by form, and prescribing the structure to which a novel should conform is likely to be doctrinaire or uninformatively vague. Something of this applies to the case study: Much of its substance is in the telling, and so we do not wish the proposals made here to be taken in a rigid or formulaic fashion.

Yet the case study is also an established research method. As well as in psychoanalysis and clinical psychology, it is used in biomedical disciplines and a variety of behavioral, social, clinical, and applied sciences, indeed anywhere a complex phenomenon is so embedded in its context that it is best, perhaps can only be, studied in that context (Bromley, 1986). Because such phenomena are extended in time and change over time (think of the analytic case), a narrative description is required of the unfolding events that make up the phenomenon under investigation.

The scientific function of the analytic case study implies a form for its reporting. As with all reports of scientific studies, the report should have a structure that reflects the logic and nature of scientific investigation. Scientific investigation—really just an expression of the scientific attitude—should be systematic, transparent, and self-critical. Thus the reporting of the case should be: systematic, to convey the maximum amount of information about the case to the reader in terms to which other practitioners have access; transparent, in that the reported facts and the inferential processes of the analyst-researcher should be as clear and as explicit as possible and the concepts used to link the material to theory should be defined as sharply as possible; and self-critical —the researcher needs to argue for the theoretical approach taken in explaining the case and justify what he does against other possible explanations and other plausible inferences that the material might yield. The implications of this are spelled out in more detail below.

Freud's comment that "psychoanalysis . . . is a method of research" (Freud, 1913) is sometimes taken to mean that simply doing psychoanalysis is research. However, this ignores the public, open nature of science and the requirement that, in order to be scientific, research needs to be presented in a form shared by a community of scholars. So while the analysis of the patient is the basis of research, it only becomes research proper when it is articulated and communicated to others in the public language and with the defined concepts of psychoanalytic theory—however problematic the terms of psychoanalysis may be at times.

One of the several challenges the analyst-in-training faces when writing up a case study is the feeling that it is an academic chore incongruent with therapeutic work. After all, training analysts spend much time getting the novice simply *to be* in the analytic hour, listening, rather than trying to help the patient, apply psychoanalytic theory, or make interpretations. But there are also other levels of listening and grasping the patient's inner world. We write here in the conviction that the analyst needs to add reflective and explanatory skills to his clinical skills in order to be a complete analyst and that becoming a full-fledged analyst demands that the student understand and be able to articulate the concepts, theories, and specific perceptions that underpin his analytic functioning in the clinical setting. In other words, the kind of effort involved in writing a case study is probably the best way there is of coming to understand what is going on in the treatment.

Although the resolution of these matters is not the subject of this paper, psychoanalysts need to be aware that the clinical case study is controversial in some parts of the scientific world. The case study, so identified with psychoanalysis, has been singled out for attack by philosophers and scientists critical of psychoanalysis (Grünbaum, 1993). Many researchers who look for an objective means of investigating human action, including psychotherapy and the theories on which it relies, believe that science is not concerned with the single case and that this excludes the case study. A common reaction to this, sometimes by psychoanalysts defending their method (Hoffman, 1991) or by others who also reject what they see as the narrow positivism in these criticisms (Denzin & Lincoln, 2000), has been to argue that the case study is a special, perhaps non-scientific, means of investigation that yields a special kind of knowledge belonging to a domain separate from orthodox scientific knowledge. This argument often takes the form that science consists of objective fact, while specifically human knowledge is about individually or socially constructed meanings—a theme that is widely discussed in the metatheoretical literature of psychoanalysis and psychology. One of the authors has argued elsewhere that this radical account of knowledge is neither necessary for, nor even relevant to, maintaining the focus on meaning in psychotherapy (Mackay, 1989, 2003a, 2003b). It is worth noting, moreover, that in this context a single case is not the same as a single instance. A theoretical prediction may be instanced many times in a single-case study that covers a period of time and a large number of events.

This bears on the reporting conventions of the case study because it is only if the case study is a form of scientific investigation that it need conform to the scientific research report structure. The position taken here[1] is that the single-case study is neither inherently non-scientific nor in need of justification by appeal to theories of special and distinct kinds of human knowledge and truth: It is an objective and legitimate type of research. It is aimed at supporting theory by exemplifying it in a case and by showing that theory can bring coherence to the apparently disparate elements of patient behavior and symptoms. This is less than a means of directly proving theory or giving decisive test to hypotheses—a position argued for in psychoanalysis by Edelson (1985, 1986a, 1986b) and by others outside the field (Yin, 1994)—and the journeyman case study done by the analyst-in-training is even further from full theory-testing research. Nonetheless, the case study is a part of the general scientific process of examining the implications, applicability, and viability of theory. Accordingly, it must be carried out and reported in a way that provides the reader maximum access to the case facts and the inferential procedures of the investigator. To conform to the central aims and procedures of scientific research, it must include a comprehensive report of the data (case narrative, findings, and case record, perhaps in the form of process notes), specify the place the study occupies in its theoretical and research context, and give an explicit account of procedure and methods, including working definitions of concepts and how they are applied.

Following upon Freud's groundbreaking studies of the Wolf Man (Freud, 1918), the Rat Man (Freud, 1909b), Dr. Schreber (Freud, 1911), Little Hans (Freud, 1909a), and other cases, subsequent innovators and original thinkers in the history of psychoanalysis have used the single-case study as a vehicle for conceptual development, introducing nascent theoretical ideas and expanding and illustrating them.[2] Analysts are guilty of sometimes treating these as if they are complete proofs of the theory. However, theoretical formulations introduced in a case study require integration with other corroborated theory and repeated successful application in a variety of contexts to count as well supported. The journeyman case study carried out by the analyst-in-training is not for introducing theory, but for applying theory to case material in order to make sense of it or bring coherence to the otherwise disparate details of a case. Or, from the reverse direction, it illustrates theory by showing how it makes sense of the material in a particularly convincing and

---

[1] A number of authors outside of the psychoanalytic realm have discussed the scientific credentials of the case study method (Bromley, 1986; Robson, 2002; Stake, 1995, 2000; Yin, 1994), leading to a revival of the sense of its scientific worth and its use in recent years.

[2] A useful anthology of such cases is to be found in Greenwald (1973). Classic and modern case histories from Freud through Kernberg are reviewed and placed in context in Schoenewolf (1990a,b).

illuminating fashion. Without conceding to any relativist views of truth and knowledge (Mackay, 2003b), we use the phrase *make sense of* rather than the stricter *explain* because the theoretical claims of the single-case study are usually empirically underdetermined and do not rule out other theoretical formulations that might also bring coherence to the same case.[3] We cannot here treat in detail the larger issue of how a case study can be scientific without providing a definitive explanation of the case. However, we can point out that the coherence of a good case account, while not sufficient for its truth, is necessary and makes the account plausible; and establishing plausibility is part of scientific investigation.

The Structure for the Case Study: Its Components and Sequence

The task of doing a single-case study has three parts; more or less sequentially these are: conceptualizing the research, carrying out the analysis and interpretation of the data, and reflecting on the results. Included in the first part, conceptualizing the study, we find three components that are formalized in the writeup: the narrative of the case, a review of the literature, and a section describing the methods and procedures that were[4] used to carry out the proposed study. This introductory section sets out and gives context to the questions driving the research project: What am I studying? How have others tried to explain the kind of presentation, behavior, and dynamics I met with in my patient? What concepts and ideas will I use to situate my patient's behavior in a theoretical framework? How will I collect relevant data from the flow of the patient's material in sessions? How will I analyze, interpret, and make inferences from the data that I collect?

The second part of the study is the systematic recounting of the results (findings), put into a section named Findings, yielded by carrying out the process of investigation as described in the first part. And in the third part, the discussion, the researcher reflects on the implications and significance of the results for the research questions set out in the

---

[3]As an illustration of this in Hunter (1994), the same case was presented in a supervisory session to 11 well-known psychoanalysts, each of whom constructed the dynamics of the case using significantly different concepts and formulations.

[4]As might be expected, if the analyst is setting out a research proposal, the tense is in the future; if reporting, it is in the past tense.

first part. That is, to what extent do my results answer my research question(s)? As discussed below, findings can be presented in a summary form followed by a more detailed discussion showing how interpretive results were derived from the material of the sessions, how inferences to the unconscious were made, and how the overall psychodynamic picture of the case came into focus as a result of the study.

In outline, the structure we are proposing[5] includes the following components:

> *Introduction*
> *Narrative*
> *Review of Literature*, including statements of the *Significance of the Study* and of the *Research Question*, which may have their own subsections and subheadings, and which are given at the close of the review.
> *Method*, including *Definitions* and *Procedures*, which may have their own subsections and subheadings
> *Findings*
> *Discussion*

The Components

INTRODUCTION

A case study often starts with a brief statement of the purpose of the study, but does not anticipate too many of the details of the later sections. Freud prefaces his case studies of the Rat Man (1909b), Schreber (1911), and the Wolf Man (1918) with a section of brief introductory remarks that serve to set the stage for the narrative, or case history, which immediately follows. In these remarks, Freud typically situates himself in relation to the patient or the case material and points the reader to noteworthy features of the case. As with an abstract, an intro-

---

[5] We are treating the case study as a special instance of the more general research report that may be seen in documents such as the *Publication Manual of the American Psychological Association* (American Psychological Association, 2001), a common standard format for research writing.

[6] For the sake of brevity, we omit such elements as *Cover Page, Acknowledgments, Abstract, References,* and *Appendices* that will also be a part of the final format of a case study written up as part of the requirements for graduation from a training institute. See for example Meadow & Bernstein (1999).

duction of this kind may well be written in retrospect, when the overall trajectory of the study has become clear.

Narrative

The two questions we may ask of any narrative are: How well does the narrative convey the "feel" of the patient, trace the development of dynamics over time, and depict the transference and countertransference? How well does the narrative highlight, and ultimately lead the reader to a clear recognition of, the issues that are later dealt with in the study?

The narrative is the story of the case as it unfolded in treatment. It is the introduction to the history and analysis of the patient. It should be a description of the analysis and not contain details of the inferences that one makes from the case material though it will be shaped by one's interests and any tentative explanation one holds. Theoretical or diagnostic language should be kept to a minimum at this stage. It is the purpose of the narrative to describe (rather than explain), in as vivid and objective manner as possible, the observable phenomena of the sessions that will be the subject of the research to follow. How these phenomena are to be understood is not the burden of the narrative. Typically, the narrative will recount the history of the treatment and be shaped in such a way as to lead towards a precise formulation of what behavior, interaction, puzzle, or otherwise remarkable development the researcher aims to explain or understand. One would expect, for example, that if a study is going to focus on a particular mode of defense and its ramifications, the actions and symptoms that typically exemplify this defense feature prominently in the narrative—without, of course, being explained in it.

There is a puzzle here: The narrative appears in the report before the statement of the research question and before any explanation of the features of the case. Indeed, a preliminary narrative can be told well before carrying out the main case study; an analyst is likely to be working with a case for some time before he chooses to research and report it. Nonetheless a good narrative anticipates the question to be studied. The solution is to distinguish the logic of the reporting sequence from its actual chronology in the process of discovery. The researcher often comes to the question, methods, and explanation through the process of reading, thinking about, and discussing the features of the case, and inevitably this affects how the narrative is presented. Even the most theoretically uninflected narrative is a reduced and heavily edited version of many hours of analysis and poring over process notes. The narrative that the analyst writes after researching the case is likely to be different from the one started with and to be retrospectively edited according to the results of one's research.

Modern psychoanalysis emphasizes two protagonists in the narrative: the patient and the analyst, and so what needs to be reported are the words and actions of the patient and the responses of the analyst. Among the latter are the countertransferential feelings, and sometimes behaviors, induced in the analytic setting. The focus of the narrative is, of course, the patient, and one thing that distinguishes the better narrative is that, whatever it reports of the analyst's induced feelings and even mistakes, the patient is illuminated rather than obscured by the report of the countertransference.

REVIEW OF THE LITERATURE

Most research in science, as the work of Kuhn (1970) and others has so well demonstrated, is not a completely new departure; it is "mopping up," extending, and applying the existing theory (the *paradigm* as Kuhn famously termed it) to particular issues. The same is true of the case study, especially the journeyman piece. It is the application of psychoanalytic theory to a particular case. It is indeed the illustration of the theory or, because psychoanalysis is such a labyrinth, a sub-theory, model, or theoretical metaphor, in a particular case. A good case study shows how the theory can be adapted and applied to a case, and how clinical material can be made sense of by the theory. This requires the study to be placed in the context of psychoanalytic theory and research, thereby justifying undertaking the study. It is the review that does this.

Reviewing the literature can be a challenge to the analyst. Being a research activity, it may not sit comfortably with the practical, clinical bent typical of the analyst. It should provide a coherent flow of information that: a) explains the conceptual framework of the study, b) describes general concepts and terms in this area of research, and c) examines specific works such as previous case studies—both early and recent—that provide a rationale for, and justify, one's study. The traditional literature review in the behavioral sciences is a review of the theory, the research, and the methods relevant to the study. Of course there is no sharp line between these, and the single-case study is itself a method. A practical way to start the review process is to carry out an analysis of one's initial research query—however vague and imprecise a set of questions that often is—that identifies the elements of the puzzle(s) that provoked the research interest. If, for example, the analyst is interested in a patient who both intrudes into the analyst's private life and also transgresses the boundaries of the analytic contract by, say, playing with appointment times, missing payments, misbehaving in the room, or taking over the analyst's role, then this yields a number of themes, each of which has spawned a psychoanalytic literature of theory, case work, and research. Some elements operative in this example might be: boundary, or boundary violations, and companion concepts like holding environment and containment or, depending on the feel of the patient's intrusiveness, introjection, projective identification, and envy (which leads naturally into the large Kleinian literature that further elaborates these notions). The analyst will likely be led into the literature describing the borderline patient. Taking another line, the topic raises the issue of technique and the analytic contract, and there is also a literature on this, going back to Freud. The analysis of the topic provides in effect a series of key words whose occurrence in the analytic literature may be researched. Not all the literature read will be directly relevant, but understanding that one's topic of research sits in a body of previous research and theory is central to the research process. And the purpose of the review is to situate one's topic in that body of work, justifying it as a topic of study.

It is worth saying something here about the role of metaphor. Much psychoanalytic insight is articulated in the form of metaphor, rather than simply theory. Indeed there is an extensive literature (Harré, 2000; Hesse, 1963; Leatherdale, 1974; Rothbart, 1997) arguing that metaphor and analogy (the constituents of models) are in any case integral to theory, rather than just a help in conceptualizing theorized processes. The language of object relations, for example, with its picture of objects projected, introjected, split, fused, and disintegrated, is constructed on analogy to physical events, as is even such a basic concept as psychic structure. And there are more specific metaphors that can be applied and extended to corral large amounts of otherwise wayward data; consider those of the container and psychic skin in object relations, and toxicity in the modern analytic literature. A good case study is often distinguished by a particularly apt and vivid use of a metaphor, and a turning point in the making of a case study is often the realization that a metaphor nicely fits and joins together aspects of the case that had previously been poorly integrated.

Reviewing the conceptualization and treatment of patients similar to one's own provides the opportunity to situate one's case in a framework of psychoanalytic concepts, theories, and diagnostic categories. Lengths of literature reviews differ according to the subject. The review should contain a comprehensive coverage of relevant literature, including studies that most closely explain or describe one's topic—the research problem. Those that are closest to one's topic, rationale, or procedures should be described in more detail than studies that are less directly related.

Importantly, and something that the new researcher often finds difficult to manage, the review should be a critical, evaluative analysis of the literature and not simply a collection of summaries. The reviewer is leading the reader to see why, of the variety of subtheories, models, and metaphors in the psychoanalytic corpus, this one above others is going to be the best for the case in hand. The reviewer is also justifying the study as adding to, or even filling a gap in, the literature. Why is this area of study—and one's study, in particular—important? Why should it be done?

Take, for example, a study by Kirman (1989) where the review of literature may be seen to play a key role in the entire design of the research. In this work, the author presents her review of the literature in two parts. First, a review of Freud's writings, showing that the concept of the repetition compulsion originally derived from clinical observation and was turned, in 1920, into a metapsychological construct connected with the death instinct. In the second part, reviewing the literature on this concept since Freud, the author finds that this transformation in the use of the concept involved internal contradictions and led to much confusion and controversy in the utilization and understanding of the term. She further argues that these confusions can be resolved by disentangling the clinical concept from its metatheoretical connection with the death instinct. A third chapter is then devoted to providing a consistent definition of the repetition compulsion. The final chapters of the study then proceed to discuss the applicability and usefulness of the concept in the analysis of a patient, focusing on the patient's patterns of repetition in the transference. This work was conceived from the beginning as a twofold study: first, a theoretical review of a central psychoanalytic concept, and second, a case study focusing on clinical material related to this concept. Here we can see very clearly how a thorough, critically evaluative review of the literature can give both structure and substance to the case study.

The review, like the narrative, is not the place to discuss the material of one's case although what the review covers will be shaped by one's interests. The literature review should end with a summary that situates the research case and the specific topic of investigation firmly in psychoanalytic language and thought. At this stage, it should be possible to state the significance of the proposed study insofar as it differs from, extends, or fills a gap in what has been done by other researchers. It should also be possible to give a precise formulation of the research question the study will be designed to answer.

Some indication of the question will appear at the end of the narrative. However, in the concluding section of the literature review, perhaps in a separate section of its own, a sharper formulation of the research question should be given. This component (only one or two paragraphs) consists of the question that encapsulates the central purpose or aim of the study. The formulation of the research question is usually the first milestone in the conceptualization of the research. It may come to the researcher very early in the research process, perhaps before any writing is done, or it may remain imprecise for a long while during which the details of the case are being processed and the review of the literature is carried out. How one ultimately sets out the narrative will be shaped by the question that one is investigating, and generally, one only comes to the question after a good deal of sifting through the case material and searching the literature for conceptual and theoretical perspectives that provide a suitable language for describing what one is studying. In this sense, the statement of the research question marks the culmination of a process of discovery, refinement, and comprehension.

In a study of one of the authors (Poser, 2001, 2002) the research question went unformulated for the first three years of the treatment and only came into focus as a result of an extraordinary sequence of sessions in which the patient stood at the foot of the couch, spoke of himself in the third person, called the analyst by his (the patient's) name, and expressed the wish to heal him. At first, the analyst's bewilderment could only be formulated in such terms as, what on earth is going on here? In examining these sessions in detail, the analyst came to feel that the patient was manipulating, transposing, constructing, and reconstructing his (the analyst's) identity in parallel to some progressive movement in his experience and internal image of himself. The analyst then asked the question: "How does the patient mold the analyst in order to advance the treatment?" In supervision, this question was recast in terms of the idea of creating psychic structure. This conceptualization of what was transpiring in the treatment enabled the analyst to see the connection between his subjective experience of being molded, manipulated, constructed, and transformed and the patient's unconscious creation of psychic structure within the treatment. These two processes were identical—two ways of looking at the same thing. The final formulation of the research question thus became: "How does the patient create psychic structure out of chaotic disorganization?" (Poser, 2001, pp. 31–50).

Regardless of how the research question is arrived at, it gives definition and direction to the study, situates the research at least implicitly in a recognizable conceptual framework that is grounded in the psychoanalytic literature, and sets the stage for the working definitions and procedures to be set forth in the methodology.

Another matter that sometimes presents a challenge to the analyst is the difficult matter of distinguishing clinical from research questions. In one sense, all the questions that one deals with are clinical (Sheftel, 1992). However, there are certain kinds of discourse where the analyst's interest is largely to speculate about, understand, instruct on, query, and think about the psychoanalytic process, including deep underlying themes that are going on in treatment—the typical "process" talk that goes on in a clinical seminar or case supervision. It is what analysts do most and might be called clinical discourse. Then there is the sort of talk that has a different, more specific purpose. Its aim is not to amplify, brainstorm, and speculate about what is going on in an analysis, so much as to form specific questions that are both relevant to a particular case and can in principle be answered through systematic examination of the case material. This is research discourse, albeit about clinical matters. The following summarizes some of the differences:

Some Features of Clinical and Research Questions

Clinical questions	Research questions
Are oriented toward amplifying and exploring the analysis	Tend to start as a research idea, rather than a single question. That is, are often a set of loosely related questions rather than a single focused query
May be specific or general, tend to be about technique	Usually the idea needs analyzing and refining to get to a specific, single research question
Often *why* questions, asking if the analyst has any sense of why such-and-such is happening	Often *how* questions, about how a specific process or strategy is used by a patient in the analysis to achieve some unconscious goal

Are part of process talk, heightening the awareness of the dynamics of the analysis, adding the experience of the others in the group	When fully refined, the research questions are not impossibly deep, i.e., do not attempt to be questions about the fundamental theoretical processes that are in any case assumed in analysis
Being exploratory, do not necessarily require answers, hence do not strictly need to be answerable	Require answers, hence need to be answerable
No requirement that the focus is on the observable	Tend to be focused on the observable processes of therapy, looking for indicators of some (hypothesized) unconscious process
No requirement that the concepts are operationally defined, as long as they can be understood	Use operationalized concepts, i.e., are clear enough to allow a method where unobservable processes may be taken to occur when specific observable events happen
No requirement that they be systematic	About those unconscious processes that may be systematically inferred from the observable
Not necessarily focused	Focused

METHOD

The purpose of this section is to describe what in the observed material is to count as an instance of the specific unconscious process, psychological state, or theoretical concept that it is held to exemplify. What will constitute data and how will it be identified and collected from the flow of material in the sessions?[7] It is precisely here that psychoanalytic theory must be linked to observation. This can best be accomplished by setting out operational, or working, definitions of the clinical phenomena under investigation. What specific meanings does one give to the diagnostic or theoretical terms used to describe the patient's symptoms, behavior, or communications? How are the key concepts that give

---

[7]The importance of this question and the related issue of what constitutes evidence in psychoanalytic research is taken up in an illuminating article by Boesky (2002).

184 □ *NIGEL MACKAY & STEVEN POSER*

direction to the study to be connected to the observables to be found in the room with the patient?

In the Poser study (2001, 2002) cited above, the question about creating psychic structure in the analysis could not be investigated directly because the concept of psychic structure in psychoanalysis has no clear-cut empirical meaning. It is indeed a metaphor. Even from a purely theoretical point of view, the concept has no universally agreed-upon meaning, as was discovered in searching the literature. The procedure devised to study this question began with the recognition that what was being studied was a dynamic situation—tracing the development of a process over time. On the basis of sifting and sorting through many detailed process notes, three "axes of observation" (Poser, 2002, pp. 265–66) were laid out that associated specific phenomena observable in sessions with three conceptual categories of particular relevance to the idea of psychic structure. Under each of these headings followed an inventory of observable material, explicitly enumerating what would count as instances or examples of, e.g., fragmentation, communications demonstrating concern with the boundaries of the self, or expressions of the patient's involvement with an externally situated transference object. These listings of observable material were intended to be as empirically objective as possible so that there was maximal transparency as to what in the observable behavior of the patient (and in the analyst's induced states) would be counted as an instance, example, or demonstration of the theoretically-described phenomenon, process, or state that it was being taken to exemplify.

To illustrate, the three axes of observation in the Poser study were given as follows:

(1) Material that exemplifies or demonstrates fragmentation and/or integration of thinking, affective, and neuro-muscular processes.

Observable material includes: confusional states, squashing, blocking, going blank or attacking thoughts or the associative links between them, the pattern and mode of the eruption of feeling, states of rapid speech and other changes of voice, breathing, bodily tension, or movement, and the connection or disconnection of affect to ideational content. Countertransference states associated with this range of symptoms include the analyst's becoming confused or dissociated, going to sleep, experiencing the patient as an automaton, or becoming preoccupied with unusual disruptions of the analyst's mind, body, or feeling states.

(2) Material that exemplifies or demonstrates concern with the boundaries of the self, the contents of the self, the representation of the self,

the sense of personal identity, and the cohesion of the body and the mind.

Observable material includes: any communication having to do with sorting out internal components of the mind or body, behaviors such as hoarding, food-grabbing, and cannibalism, any communication having to do with what is me as opposed to not-me, the demarcation of the inner world as opposed to the outer world, and any material having to do with the representation, appearance, identity, and coherence of the patient's mind or body. Countertransference states associated with this range of symptoms include any experience of the patient as a marionette, a conglomeration of parts, disparate voices or personae, any experience of having lost something or of being empty, full, or of the analyst's speaking, thinking, or feeling out of an alien, confused, or fragmented sense of his own identity.

(3) Material that exemplifies or demonstrates the state of the patient's involvement with objects experienced or described as external to the self.

Observable material includes: states of object-relatedness and their fluctuations in the session—when and how he demonstrates awareness of himself in relation to another locus of thought and feeling outside himself, instances of confusion as to who did, said, felt, or thought what, and any verbal or behavioral evidence of introjective or projective processes in the construction of the analyst as a transference object. Countertransference states associated with this range of symptoms include the analyst's sense of whether he is being spoken to as a separate object or being obliterated, the analyst's misidentifying which of the therapist and patient said, thought, or did what, or any unusual states of merging in which the analyst felt himself having or verbalizing the patient's thoughts or feelings, or any experiences of being conjoined, internalized, or externalized by the patient, either mentally or physically. (pp. 265–66)

This methodology was designed so that the researcher could, in principle, track the functioning of the patient's apparatus of awareness, the evolution of his representation of himself, and of his progressive construction of the analyst. From this scheme, it was then possible to provide a working definition of psychic structure, the key term in the research question and of the study as a whole, viz.:

For such a patient to be able to have thoughts, to have feelings, to connect one to another in meaningful ways, and to be able to put these into language, to have clearly differentiated boundaries between himself and the outside world, and to be able to experience himself as a coherent unity of mind and body in relation to objects and persons outside himself in an aware, purposeful, and feelingful way, is for him to have acquired the fundamental rudiments of psychic structure (Poser, 2002, pp. 266–7).

Other key terms in the conceptual framework of the study deriving from modern psychoanalytic theory, e.g., ego-field and object-field of the mind, played a crucial role in the formulation of the findings and were defined at that stage (Poser, 2002, pp. 282–83).

PROCEDURES

In this section, the researcher describes how the study was carried out, that is, how he or she selected, organized, parsed, and examined the data. The psychoanalyst makes inferences from surface phenomena (actions, words, symptoms, associations, induced feelings) to the unconscious processes that drive them. Making these links as explicit as possible meets a requirement of proper scientific research mentioned above, i.e., of being transparent: rendering the inferential processes of the analyst-researcher as clearly and as explicitly as possible and defining the concepts used to link the material to theory as sharply as possible. In the Poser study, a great deal of the patient's most significant material was presented in the form of dreams and nonverbal, symbolic enactments. Therefore, much of the analytic, inferential work was devoted to the interpretation of these indirect and symbolic communications, along with the continuing analysis of countertransference states, thoughts, perceptions, and feelings induced in the analyst in the course of treatment. These inferential, interpretive processes are recounted in the discussion section of the study.

FINDINGS

This is equivalent to the results section of the traditional research report with the difference that in a single-case study, one generally does not have the option of presenting a list of statistics and tables that summarizes the results. Case-study data, being qualitative, is compendious and very hard to reduce and tabulate without losing much of the texture. On the other hand, putting large amounts of data in the main body of a report threatens to overwhelm the rest of the presentation. Yet transparency requires that it be made as available as possible to other scholars. One way to manage one's findings is to put the bulk of the data in an appendix at the back of the work and in the findings section to present a summary of the results derived, using extracts from and references to material that can be further examined in the appendix if needed. The data will have been analysed, interpreted, and distilled in the formulation of one's findings; the inferential, interpretive, reflective process of arriving at those findings will be the subject of the discussion chapter to follow. Even the bulk data of the appendix—process notes or other means for recording case observations—may not comprise all the data collected, but merely representative selections from perhaps hundreds of sessions.

In the Poser (2002) study, the findings are presented in a two-page section (pp. 267–68) that directly proposes an answer to the research question in terms of the evolution and progression of transference states the patient unconsciously enacted in the treatment. Four phases of this progressive structuring are then described. This brief statement of an answer to the research question is then followed by a detailed analytical study of each successive phase in the treatment, highlighting and interpreting particular behaviors, interactions, dreams, and other symbolic communications that give substance to the central claims outlined in the findings. This detailed exposition of the movement in the treatment corresponding to the structuralizing process in the patient's mind constitutes the discussion of the study (Poser, 2002, pp. 268–82).

DISCUSSION

We propose that the interpretation of the data be put into the discussion, where one reviews for the reader the study's purpose and hypothesis and shows how the findings may be understood as answering the question that was set in the earlier stage of the work. It is in the discussion that the analyst interprets the data, making explicit the inferential processes whereby meanings are derived from the manifest content of the patient's symptoms, communications, and enactments. Note, however, that this is different from what is recommended elsewhere (Meadow & Bernstein, 1999), where much of what we suggest placing in the discussion is included in the findings. The uncertainty on this matter derives from the fact that the inferential, interpretive processes of the single-case study, being qualitative, are usually more elaborate. That is, going from results to claims of support or otherwise for one's hypothesis is more complex. The question arises: Where should the reports of this be placed? The answer has to do with convention and convenience rather than any methodological principle.

However, it seems reasonable, for example, to put into the discussion such material as the following extended extract from one of the early sessions reported in the Poser (2001) study, together with the analyst's inferences and interpretations:

> In our eighth session, which was dominated by the motif of self-crip-pling, Joseph reported that the brakes on his car were shot, that he can't stop the car at red lights, and thinks he could get into a serious accident. He asked himself whether he should spend the money to fix the brakes or spend it on prostitutes. He said it was a value judgment. Then he reported a dream of having two heads, a type of dream he has had many times before. One of the heads belongs to "Joseph"—an evil, insane, internal figure he spoke of in the third person, even though this is the patient's given name. "Joseph" lives inside him. "When Joseph takes over," he said, "it's like a steel claw comes down on me." In another dream, he saw a scarecrow figure with a traffic-light head. "Red light, green light," I said. "Yes," he replied, then continued, "If, on the other hand, I had a heart full of love . . ." He never finished the sentence. He stopped speaking abruptly. His breathing changed. There were three or four minutes of silence. I waited. "My mind went blank," he said, ". . . that was significant." "What was significant?" I asked. "My mind went blank. I couldn't continue. My breathing changed." He then contin-ued at his more usual rapid, non-stop pace. He said he went to a strip joint on 42nd Street last week but the place was closed. "Yes!" he exclaimed (quite loudly, sounding like "Eureka!") "God forbid an attractive woman should talk to me!" (p.7)

At this point, the analyst's interpretive thought processes were given as follows:

> From what I already knew, the arousal of erotic feelings is experienced by him as very dangerous. They can be (unconsciously) converted direct-ly into hate and violent impulses and this has resulted in his assaulting women he found sexually attractive. They make him nauseous. He wants to punch them. He has also reported feeling like telling them, "If you don't love me, I'll kill you," which I myself experienced as an unspoken but fundamental premise of the treatment contract: that if I don't love him, he will kill me and that if I don't save him, he will kill himself. The arousal of libidinal feelings is dangerous because it is so closely related to the explosion of rage. The conversion of arousal into hatred is uncon-scious and reveals how the patient's libidinal and aggressive drives are conjoined in a pathological fusion, with the aggressive assuming domi-nance even, or especially, when the stimulus is libidinal. But this creates

enormous anxiety and tension in him, which he has no means of discharging except to confuse or obliterate his psychic presence in the moment, becoming outwardly chaotic while withdrawing behind a wall of heavily insulated, autistic solitude. When the patient exclaimed, "Yes! God forbid an attractive woman should talk to me!" I was able, after reflection on this episode, to hear him as saying, "Yes! God forbid I should lose control of myself and try to kill somebody!" (p. 8)

At a later stage in the study, this episode of the patient's "going blank" was used to illustrate a key element in his defense organization—psychic fragmentation as a defense against psychotic disintegration. Here, in the discussion, Joseph's going blank was interpreted as exemplifying a "mental and emotional shutting down—an unconscious reduction to psychic blankness in response to the arousal of dangerous feelings, such as emotional longing, sexual arousal, or rage" (pp. 123–24).

Many other examples could be chosen, but the key to transparency in the building of a psychoanalytic understanding of a case is in making the interpretive, inferential processes as explicit as possible so that, in the end, not only does the construal of the clinical phenomena make the best possible sense, but that the thought process that brought one there is clear, evident, and defensible in its own right.

The Publication Manual of the American Psychological Association (American Psychological Association, 1974) sums up the purpose of the discussion as well as we can:

After presenting the results, you are in a position to evaluate and interpret their implications . . . with respect to your original hypothesis. In the Discussion section, you are free to examine, interpret, and qualify the results, as well as to draw inferences from them. Emphasize any theoretical consequences of the results and the validity of your conclusions. . . .

Open the discussion with a clear statement of the support or nonsupport for your original hypothesis. Similarities and differences between your results and the work of others should clarify and confirm your conclusions. . . .

Identifying the practical and theoretical implications of your study, suggesting improvements on your research, or proposing new research may be appropriate, but keep these comments brief. In general, be guided by these questions:

• What have I contributed here?
• How has my study helped to resolve the original problem?
• What conclusions and theoretical implications can I draw from my study?

The responses to these questions are the core of your contribution, and readers have a right to clear, unambiguous, and direct answers. (pp. 27–28)

Conclusion

If psychoanalysts are serious about the scientific and systematic nature of the case study—understanding that science is not to be taken in the narrow way it often is in the behavioral sciences—then we need to ground investigative procedures in scientific epistemology and to keep the means for reporting them in line with scientific practice. We have in this paper tried to show how this may be done without losing the rich qualitative value of the case study. We have presented for the case study a rationale and structure that conforms to that of the traditional research paper, making sure the investigative methods and inferential procedures are systematic and transparent and the reporting is self-critical.

REFERENCES

American Psychological Association (1974), *Publication Manual of the American Psychological Association,* Third Edition. Washington, DC: American Psychological Association.

—— (2001), *Publication Manual of the American Psychological Association,* Fifth Edition. Washington, DC: American Psychological Association.

Boesky, D. (2002), Why don't our institutes teach methodology of clinical psychoanalytic evidence? *Psychoanalytic Quarterly,* 71:445–475.

Bromley, D. B. (1986), *The Case-Study Method in Psychology and Related Disciplines.* New York: John Wiley.

Denzin, N. K. & Y. S. Lincoln (2000), Introduction: The discipline and practice of qualitative research. *The Handbook of Qualitative Research.* Second Edition. N. K. Denzin & Y. S. Lincoln, eds. Thousand Oaks, CA: Sage Publications.

Edelson, M. (1985), The hermeneutic turn and the single case study in psychoanalysis. *Psychoanalysis & Contemporary Thought,* 8(4):567–614.

———— (1986a), Causal explanation in science and in psychoanalysis: implications for writing a case study. *Psychoanalytic Study of the Child*, 41:89–127.

———— (1986b), The evidential value of the psychoanalyst's clinical data. *Behavioral & Brain Sciences*, 9(2):232–234.

Freud, S. (1909a), Analysis of a phobia in a five-year-old boy. *Standard Edition*. London: Hogarth Press, 10:1–150.

———— (1909b), Notes upon a case of obsessional neurosis. *Standard Edition*. London: Hogarth Press, 10:151–250.

———— (1911), Psychoanalytic notes on an autobiographical account of a case of paranoia (dementia paranoides). *Standard Edition*. London: Hogarth Press, 12:1–79.

———— (1913), On psycho-analysis. *Standard Edition*. London: Hogarth Press, 12:205–212.

———— (1918), From the history of an infantile neurosis. *Standard Edition*. London: Hogarth Press, 10:1–124.

Greenwald, H. (1973), *Great Cases in Psychoanalysis*. Northvale, NJ: Jason Aronson.

Grünbaum, A. (1993), *Validation in the Clinical Theory of Psychoanalysis: A Study in the Philosophy of Psychoanalysis*. Madison, CT: International Universities Press.

Harré, R. (2000), Varieties of theorizing and the project of psychology. *Theory & Psychology*, 10(1):57–62.

Hesse, M. B. (1963), *Models and Analogies in Science*. London: Sheed and Ward.

Hoffman, I. Z. (1991), Discussion: toward a social constructivist view of the psychoanalytic situation. *Psychoanalytic Dialogues*, 1:74–105.

Hunter, V. (1994), *Psychoanalysts Talk*. New York: The Guilford Press.

Kirman, N. (1989), *A Critical Examination of the Concept of the Repetition Compulsion with An Illustrative Case History*. New York: Center for Modern Psychoanalytic Studies.

Kuhn, T. S. (1970), *The Structure of Scientific Revolutions*. Revised Edition. Chicago: University of Chicago Press.

Leatherdale, W. H. (1974), *The Role of Analogy, Model and Metaphor in Science*. Amsterdam: North-Holland Publishing.

Mackay, N. (1989), *Motivation and Explanation: An Essay on Freud's Philosophy of Science*. Madison, CT: International Universities Press.

———— (2003a), On "just not getting it": a reply to Macnamara and to Raskin and Neimeyer. *Theory & Psychology*, 13(3):411–419.

———— (2003b), Psychotherapy and the idea of meaning. *Theory & Psychology*, 13(3):359–386.

Meadow, P. W. & J. Bernstein (1999), *Handbook for the Final Research Project*. New York: Center for Modern Psychoanalytic Studies.

Poser, S. (2001), *Finding A Shape: The Creation of Psychic Structure in a Psychoanalytic Setting*. New York: Center for Modern Psychanalytic Studies.

────── (2002), Finding a shape: the creation of psychic structure in a psychoanalytic setting. *Modern Psychoanalysis*, 27:263–288.

Robson, C. (2002), *Real World Research: A Resource for Social Scientists and Practitioner-Researchers*. Second Edition. Cambridge, MA: Blackwell.

Rothbart, D. (1997), *Explaining the Growth of Scientific Knowledge: Metaphors, Models, and Meanings*. Lewiston, NY.: E. Mellen Press.

Schoenewolf, G. (1990a), *Turning Points in Analytic Therapy: The Classic Cases*. Northvale, NJ: Jason Aronson.

────── (1990b), *Turning Points in Analytic Therapy: From Winnicott to Kernberg*. Northvale, NJ: Jason Aronson.

Sheftel, S. (1992), Relearning the research process: on the connection between research and treatment. *Modern Psychoanalysis*, 17:203–229.

Stake, R. (1995), *The Art of Case Study Research*. Thousand Oaks, CA: Sage Publications.

────── (2000), Case studies. *The Handbook of Qualitative Research*. Second Edition. N. K. Denzin & Y. S. Lincoln, eds. Thousand Oaks, CA: Sage Publications.

Yin, R. K. (1994), *Case Study Research: Design and Methods*. Second Edition. Thousand Oaks, CA: Sage Publications.

Dep. of Psychology
University of Wollongong
Wollongong, New South Wales 2522
Australia
nmackay@vow.edu.av

P.O. Box 122
Salt Point, NY 12578
stevenposer@earthlink.net

Understanding the Fieldwork Experience: How Do We Know When Students "Get It" about Narcissism?[1]

VICKI G. SEMEL

An important contribution of modern psychoanalysis to the field of mental health treatment is its commitment to work with extremely regressed patients. To work with such a patient population depends heavily on therapists' understanding of their own reactions as well as of patients' dynamics. Training to achieve these goals is an essential aspect of becoming a professional in this field.

This paper examines the mental health fieldwork experience as described by students and faculty in two modern psychoanalytic training centers and proposes seven criteria by which the student therapist's growth in understanding the narcissistic patient can be measured. They are: the student's observation of the contact function; the student's interventions; the student's defenses and reactions to those defenses; the student's descriptions of the patient's symbolic and unconscious verbal and nonverbal communications; the student's reactions to the patient and an understanding of those reactions; the student's reactions to supervision;

[1] I would like to thank the students, psychoanalysts, and faculty who have guided this inquiry: J. Ashworth, E. Barz, A. Bolinder, S. Bradley, P. Bratt, J. Cohen, C. Harte, N. Kirman, J. LaNoue Lippincott, M. Lovell, R. MacAloon, N. Mackay, B. Mancevski, R. Marshall, P. Meadow, R. Meyers, F. Newsome, M. Pumilia, R. Rode, R. Sachs, M. Sackler, R. Sperling, H. Spotnitz, R. Wein, and S. Zaretsky. Also thanks to Ilene Dorf Manahan.

the student's interactions with classmates. Vignettes that describe the criteria and a longer case study of one student's growth are also presented.

Modern psychoanalysts have been treating the more seriously disordered—for example, preoedipal, narcissistic, schizophrenic[2]—patient since Hyman Spotnitz added to Freud's theoretical perspective and introduced technical innovations to treat patients who developed a distinct type of transference, i.e., the narcissistic transference. Spotnitz's techniques were based on the belief that such patients could be treated and the narcissistic transference could be resolved. As Spotnitz (2004) explains,

> Unlike the patient functioning at the oedipal level of development, the pathologically narcissistic individual does not invariably relate to the analyst as a separate and distinct person. In their relationship, the schizophrenic patient transfers feelings that he developed for himself as well as for others during the first two years of life. He may also confuse the analyst's feelings with his own. In short, a two-way emotional transaction is revived and communicated as originating in one locale—the mind of the patient. That transaction, suggestive of a re-experiencing of the ego in the process of formation, is identified as narcissistic transference. (p. 129)

Freud (1914) initially thought of narcissism as a self-loving phenomenon. He concluded that patients with narcissistic neuroses withdrew from the world and turned their libidinal impulses toward themselves. This theory developed before the early 1920s, when Freud (1920) added an understanding of the aggressive drive and then focused on the dual drive theory in which aggression and libido produce forces that shape an individual's perceptions and personality structure. Yet Freud did not re-examine his view of narcissistic neuroses in terms of this dual drive theory. He believed that narcissistic patients could not be treated successfully because they could not establish a transference with the analyst, instead expressing indifference or hatred. Freud (1933) remained convinced of the impossibility of treating the narcissistic neuroses, patients whose primitive ways of relating did not make them amenable to positive transference and resistance analysis (p. 155). Freud's (1917, 1933) belief that these patients could not be influenced through interpretation remained his position throughout his life.

---

[2]In this paper, "preoedipal" and "narcissistic" are used interchangeably. Schizophrenia is a subtype of the general category of preoedipal and narcissistic disorders.

Spotnitz (1976b, c) concluded, with the benefit of the dual drive theory, that narcissism is actually self-*hatred* used to protect the idea of the object by turning feelings of aggression and self-hate toward oneself in what is conceptualized as the narcissistic defense. To Spotnitz (2004), despite the fact that the patient with a narcissistic transference withdraws behind a wall, a "stonewall of narcissism," the patient is seen as one who *can* be helped to develop more mature coping patterns.

Spotnitz's (2004) straightforward conclusion that it is possible to work through the narcissistic transference and then the object transference is complemented by the emotional reality he describes of being with such patients. This experience is especially relevant for the beginning psychoanalytic student. In such an environment, a therapist may experience reactions of fear, disorientation, discomfort, frustration, anger, and incompetence; these are natural reactions. A beginning analyst, especially a novice in training, can act on feelings that are induced by the interaction with the patient. The therapist's training will help him understand the reactions he is experiencing or defending against so he can work with the patient to make use of the narcissistic transference as it develops. The purpose of modern psychoanalytic training is to enable the therapist and the patient to accept these and all inductions.

In his "Trends in Modern Psychoanalytic Supervision," Spotnitz (1976a) presented three goals of supervision. The first is to increase the student's understanding of a patient's psychodynamics. The second is to "help the student tolerate the feelings induced in him by the patient . . . and to use those feelings to facilitate the progress of the case," recognizing that the student often represses those feelings rather than accept them because "feelings appear to be connected with tendencies in the student himself" (p. 2). And third is to help the therapist communicate in an appropriate fashion with the patient. The difficulties for the therapist in working successfully with the schizophrenic patient are described as the reason such treatment is often rejected for patients who can indeed benefit from the treatment (Karon, 1992).

What adds to the difficulty of such work is that the narcissistic patient does not see boundaries between himself and the outside. It is then a critical growth step for the modern analyst to realize that he is not being seen as a separate person. The therapist learns to accept that not being seen as a separate individual, but as an extension of—or as one with—the patient is a natural part of the experience. Recognizing that with the narcissistic patient there is "one person alone in the room," how does the therapist react and what does the therapist say or not say to the patient?

Becoming familiar with the concept of the narcissistic defense (Spotnitz, 1976b, c) is a useful addition to the therapist's understanding of the preoedipal patient. Such a concept helps the therapist understand the patient as protecting the idea of another, the therapist, from bottled-up aggression by turning this aggression against the patient's own ego. Deciphering the communications of a narcissistic patient also enables the beginning therapist to step back somewhat from emotionally frustrating and confusing interactions to understand that the patient is talking largely to him- or herself symbolically; that is what we mean by "alone in the room."

"Alone in the room" is a difficult concept to accept. As Meadow (1991) describes, it is challenging for the therapist to understand the narcissistic nonverbal or symbolic communication and to experience the patient as in an objectless world. How, then, can we as psychoanalytic researchers describe this world so we can educate our students to the differences between patients who are in an object-oriented state from those who are tied to narcissism?

Much of the psychoanalytic literature ignores these problems while expressing a concern with training the well-selected patient and therapist. And while there has been concern with issues around candidate training, the initial attention set a high bar for the analytic candidate's character and functioning during the selection process (Waelder, 1961; Heimann, 1968). Much discussion centered on the separation of the training analysis from evaluation of the candidate's progress (Fleming & Weiss, 1978; Wallerstein, 1978) since the first approach to training had enlisted the training analyst as an evaluator of the student. Frustrations with the conflicts between a training analysis and a therapeutic analysis were reviewed by Simenauer (1983). A more recent description suggested placing the secondary analysis in a secondary place since its role with candidates may be too inhibiting (Thoma, 1993). Wallerstein (1978) reviewed the views of psychoanalytic institutes according to training and admissions standards and found enormous variability on selection processes and details of training. The importance of supervision in evaluating progress of candidates was also recommended (Fleming & Weiss, 1978).

The training of candidates, once they are accepted into candidate status, has come into question. The issue of assessing a student's progress is important (Fleming & Weiss, 1978). Dealing with the problem candidate is a more recent concern (Weiss, 1982), raising the issue of whether the candidate is inappropriate for training with perhaps too much of his own narcissism or whether the patient was inappropriately selected and is too disturbed for traditional analysis.

In a series of articles, Kernberg (2000a, 2000b, 1996, 1986) expressed some frustration with the institutional rigidity of psychoanalytic education. He claimed that the institutions quashed creativity and operated more as vehicles for indoctrination, concluding that the training was more a technical education and a religious indoctrination.

In this literature, there is very little written about effectively "learning" how to treat narcissistic patients. In fact, the goal of the initial stages of training and treatment in these articles is to assess narcissism as a basis for excluding the student or patient from involvement in the analytic process. As such, much of the focus in the traditional literature on training and supervision seems to value the well-functioning candidate and patient as a prerequisite for the psychoanalytic experience.

And while there have been psychoanalytic clinicians, such as Rosenfeld (1987), Kernberg (1975, 1986), Kohut (1971), and Searles (1965), working to treat these more regressed patients, the literature on training therapists to treat these more regressed patients is more a focus of modern psychoanalysts. The modern psychoanalytic literature on training accepts the present functioning of the student and/or patient and begins the training process. A commitment to study training as both content and emotional processes has existed since the early literature in modern psychoanalysis (e.g., Spotnitz, 1976; Hanigsberg, 1978; Margolis, 1978; Meadow & Clevans, 1978).

So while we have the academic literature on the subject, the question remains: How do we know when the student "gets it"? How do we know that the student is "learning" how to be with and understand the narcissistic patient? What indications do we have that the student understands the myriad issues related to working with the narcissistic patient? Can we identify students that "get it" as opposed to those who do not (at least do not yet get it) and therefore should be receiving more training to work with the narcissistic patient?

The Fieldwork Experience and Its Impact

Modern psychoanalysis has made singular contributions in the field of treating preoedipal patients. In addition to concluding that such patients can be treated, modern psychoanalysis has taught therapists how to work with patients by learning to tolerate and deal with the reactions induced in the therapist (Ross, 1976). Ultimately, both the patient and the therapist can be helped to experience the powerful feelings of the narcissistic transference relationship.

The development of a modern psychoanalyst who can be with the seriously regressed patient is an especially challenging and emotionally intense course of study; it takes years of psychoanalytic growth through personal analysis, supervision, and academic coursework. The modern analytic commitment to working with these primitive patients is a critically important part of a modern analyst's training.

Modern analytic institutes have implemented fieldwork as an essential component in a student's education. Only after a number of courses and participation in one's own psychoanalysis can a student opt to begin the exciting and oft-dreaded fieldwork. During this introductory clinical phase of their training, students experience the reality of being with regressed individuals in a protected mental health environment, in either a mental hospital or a day treatment center. For most students, this proves to be a watershed activity in their training, deepening their understanding of how to be with patients syntonically.

My work at the Academy of Clinical and Applied Psychoanalysis (ACAP), based in West Orange, NJ, and the Center for Modern Psychoanalytic Studies (CMPS) in New York City, accredited institutes that train clinicians to deal effectively with regressed patients, provided the basis for study of the three-semester externship program, which involves a fieldwork placement, clinical case courses, small group supervision, and the continuation of one's personal analysis as well as other relevant coursework. The unique growth that occurs during the fieldwork phase remains an integral part of the student's approach to all patients.

While many teachers and supervisors devote themselves to the growth of their students and have a "feeling" for their maturation in the field, it is difficult to describe in more clinical terms what the teacher is "seeing." Most teachers have a sense of when that training is complete enough to encourage the student to move onto the next level, the consultation center level, when the private practice model for treatment of individual patients begins. However, it would be useful to begin a dialogue on what we as teachers—and as students—believe are the goals during this first period of clinical training.

The purpose of this paper is to determine, through the application of specific clinical criteria, if we can tell whether a student understands the preoedipal patient and can successfully create a comfortable, ego-syntonic environment for the patient. It is *not* a paper on training students to work with difficult patients, but is designed to help consider the outcomes of the initial clinical part of training and to ascertain whether a student is both academically and emotionally ready to be with the preoedipal patient on the next clinical level of training.

To analyze a student therapist's "readiness" and develop these criteria, I reviewed the first stage of the clinical training to operationalize how students understand the preoedipal patient as well as themselves in relation to the patient. I then crafted a set of categories that might enable both students and teachers to look at their work together to see whether the fieldwork experience is helping the student develop the professional skills and tools that are the goals of modern analytic training.

Further, I interviewed experienced psychoanalysts, teachers, and supervisors who have taught students in fieldwork level courses and/or who have been fieldwork students to learn what convinced them that students are ready to move on in their coursework. Second, I studied students in a fieldwork class at ACAP to determine whether their orientation to their patients shifted during the year. To accomplish this objective and to examine the important concepts, I reviewed students' process notes, papers, and comments in class discussions and noted my observations of their interactions with their classroom colleagues. From their work, I was able to see how students changed and grew in the course of their fieldwork experience. What had changed? What went on in class? What did we notice about students that led us to conclude that they were functioning well and could work "modern analytically" with difficult patients? What criteria might we then consider in determining professional skill?[3]

An Examination of the Student Therapist's Growth in Being Able to Sit with and Understand the Narcissistic Patient: Criteria

If the unique aspect of modern psychoanalytic education is to help students work with preoedipal patients, what criteria can we use to determine whether the student has gained the necessary knowledge and understanding to work with these patients? During the externship/fieldwork assignment, students may experience a variety of dynamics and have a variety of reactions to these dynamics. As supervisors and teachers, we can encourage them to talk about patients and their interactions and, through supervisory guidance and classroom teaching, help students grow in the course of and as a result of their fieldwork experience.

[3]The ACAP Externship Manual for the Paper and Presentation, developed in cooperation with Marcia Pumilia and Sheila Zaretsky (2004), provided a jumping off point for this paper.

From my interviews with teachers, supervisors, and students who have completed the fieldwork experience and graduated and from my own observations in the classroom, I proffer seven discussion points to determine a student's skills and comfort in dealing with the preoedipal patient. With each of the seven criteria, I offer vignettes gleaned from my interviews and observations that illustrate the respective point. Then, I present a detailed example of one student's treatment of a narcissistic patient, drawing upon the student's externship paper and presentation.

The seven criteria are neither self-contained nor mutually exclusive. While they often overlap, they seem to serve as good benchmarks as we strive to determine whether a student has acquired some of the skills useful in treating narcissistic patients. At the very least, I would hope the proposal of these criteria might open a dialogue that will help us identify qualities useful in the treatment of narcissistic patients.

The Student's Observation of the Contact Function

This concept is based on the idea that the patient knows the amount of input or stimulation he can tolerate and teaches the therapist this by how he withdraws or approaches the therapist with words and enactments. The goal is for the student to follow the narcissistic patient's contact—for example, his/her questioning of the therapist. This would be in opposition to the therapist's reacting, as a result of his or her own discomfort, by talking too much, coming late to a session, ending a session early, or generally acting on feelings of anxiety, fear, or anger generated by the patient. Can and does the student follow the patient's lead in initiating communication? Is the student sensitive to the cues the patient gives about the amount of stimulation he wants from the therapist, and is the student able to comfortably regulate his input in response to the patient's lead?

> Having learned to be quiet and follow the patient's lead, Mrs. B, an experienced social worker, found she learned much more about her patients by being quiet and listening and by not intruding in their flow. By waiting even a few additional seconds before commenting, she found patients talk more. One of her fieldwork patients was making no contact at all, so Mrs. B became equally quiet. By mirroring the patient, she found the patient improved in his ability to talk. She then noticed that he began talking about one topic and then shifted into a discussion of the details of his making copies on Xerox machines. Mrs. B saw this as a way for him

to avoid too much tension, and as she learned to follow the patient's lead, not her own internal state, she began to think of his communications as symbolic communication.

The Student's Interventions

How does the student therapist respond to the patient? Through following the patient's contact functioning, does he perceive whether and how the patient is expressing his own state and whether the patient sees the therapist as his emotional twin or as "an objectless phenomenon"? Is the student's intervention based upon his understanding of the patient, or is the student reacting to a countertransference aroused by the patient's primitive state? Do the student's interventions demonstrate an understanding of the patient's primitive state, or is the therapist overcome by and resistant to the countertransference? Does the student recognize that the patient considers the therapist to be in the room with him for a two-way "conversation," or does the student perceive the patient as "alone in the room" and talking to part of his mind? Does the therapist react to the relationship the patient establishes by discussing what the patient is talking about in the room, or is the therapist pursuing a discussion of what the patient is doing or not doing outside the room? Is the therapist able to sit quietly and be "out of contact" with the patient, or does he feel the uncontrollable need to talk? Through his interventions, is the student's reaction helping the patient talk or simply demonstrating his own discomfort in the situation? Is the student using any or all of the following interventions: asking appropriate object-oriented questions, questions that direct the patient away from the fragmented ego into some possible curiosity about the external world or even the analyst; reflecting, by which the therapist echoes the patterns and styles of interaction of the patient, thus seeming similar to the patient; using joining techniques, which help the patient feel that the external object is agreeable and agreeing with him or his perceptions of the world; or exploring—all with care to protect the patient's ego?

A patient in fieldwork began talking about the fact that the counseling facility was planning to throw him out. Operating more from her social work background, Mrs. D, the therapist, knew this was not true. Initially she tried to reassure the patient. "Could he find out if this was true?" she asked. But then she began to hear his fear as a projection and even a wish, and developed an intervention that took into account that the narcissistic transference was all that mattered. She then wondered with the patient whether he could keep his appointments with her, even if he did not remain in the program. While she was "in the room," she was truly understanding what it means to be "alone in the room" with a patient. She noted how earlier in her training she could not describe the state with a patient except to characterize it as "just some uncomfortable alone feelings." Now she has words for the situation and feels alone in the room as if she does not exist. "I think this is the birth of a modern psychoanalyst," stated her fieldwork supervisor. "She is beginning to understand her patient's preverbal state."

The Student's Defenses and Reactions to Those Defenses

As a patient induces his regressed behaviors in the therapist, the therapist can become immersed in feeling alone and irrelevant. More experienced therapists describe a feeling of physical distance from the patient's feelings and are able to talk about those feelings. Attaining this skill is a very important step in a student's growth. Prior to achieving that level of growth, however, one might ask whether the student is aware of his own primitive feelings and impulses (countertransference) that are aroused by the patient? Does the student have and can he describe his own emotional reactions to a patient or does he express defenses against those feelings?

Considering and reacting to defenses can be approached as a three-part process. Initially, a student has his own defenses aroused by being with the patient, e.g., omnipotence. At a more advanced stage, as the student becomes immersed in feeling "non-existent" with the narcissistic patient, he might begin to feel overwhelmed, inadequate, incompetent and react with feelings of hopelessness or helplessness or by acting out with anger, rage, or even a decision to leave the field. At the most advanced level, the student develops the ability to tolerate and describe his emotional reactions to the patient, for example, inadequacy and incompetence, yet stays with the patient's feelings, however horrible or primitive.

One day in class, we were generally discussing the contact function. Mrs. S, a new student—a kind, likeable woman—spoke up about her discomfort with her patient's silence. A nursery school teacher by training, she liked to nurture and pick up the children when they are "down" and encourage and positively support them. She obviously was taking this same nurturing approach with her clients. Yet she said she noticed that she felt rejecting with some patients; she found it upsetting to admit to this reaction. She felt most rejecting of Mr. X, whom she described as a "well-dressed skeleton that sits silently and in a frozen posture in the session." To her, this state made him quite dislikable.

Yet the student felt miserable and terribly uncomfortable as she found herself disliking Mr. X more and more. During the class session, she realized that she actually wanted to get rid of Mr. X and admitted that in a previous session when he looked at his watch and asked whether the session was over, it gave her a perfect opportunity to respond in the affirmative and "get rid of him." She encouraged him to leave, ending their session 15 minutes early. Very upset about her actions and discussing them openly, the student therapist was able to acknowledge feelings that were difficult for her to have. It was apparent that some good learning had come from this experience. Furthermore, her classmates responded that they would have reacted similarly to this patient and genuinely supported her feeling state in a joining intervention that helped her to feel accepted, even though she had acted to reject the patient.

THE STUDENT'S DESCRIPTIONS OF THE PATIENT'S SYMBOLIC AND UNCONSCIOUS VERBAL AND NONVERBAL COMMUNICATIONS

The student becomes aware of what is going on in terms of the patient's unconscious communications and develops the ability to observe and describe symbolic meaning in the patient's manifest and verbal communications, as well as in symbolic, nonverbal communications or character defenses. These character defenses involve the patient's body language, posture, gestures, and indirect ways of communicating, e.g., grooming, lifestyle, odor, avoidances, fears, and regressed behaviors. Is the student also aware of the patient's treatment-destructive resistances, silences, enactments, and avoidance of expressing feelings or thoughts, or does the student/therapist become bogged down in resistances to feeling, for example, alone, dead, or irrelevant? Additionally, the student should be aware that he might be experiencing feelings induced in him by the patient. Ultimately, the student should be able to move from providing purely descriptions of the student's reactions to the patient's behaviors to becoming able to make inferences about the symbolic meaning of verbalizations, nonverbal messages, and actions. If the patient says, "The room is hot," does the student wonder if this might mean that the therapist is overstimulating the patient? If the patient says someone is mistreating him, does the student pick up that he might really be referring to the therapist? Does the student recognize that the patient's communication has a transference meaning and is not directly about the therapist? At the most advanced level, the student realizes he can learn from the patient and use the patient as a consultant—both taking information as it comes directly from the patient and eliciting input.

> A student noted that following sessions with Mr. F, a man who dressed immaculately and talked obsessively, she felt dirty and had to go wash herself and brush her teeth. After months of this pattern, she suddenly became aware that this reaction was related to the session with Mr. F and began thinking about it. Through supervision, she became aware of what might be the patient's message about himself as an induction in the therapist. She developed a hypothesis that there was something "dirty" and "disgusting" about himself that the patient had been expressing through the therapist's reaction.

The Student's Reactions to the Patient and an Understanding of Those Reactions

Does the student understand the patient's communication and the budding narcissistic transference? Is the student aware that his own primitive feelings and impulses (countertransference) are aroused by the patient? Is the patient alone in an objectless state? Has the patient developed the idea of a twin in which no difference between the patient and therapist can be tolerated? Or does the patient have some awareness of the object? This sensitivity to patient messages develops over time. The transference contributes to understanding the preoedipal transference state created by the patient in his fragmented psychic condition. The therapist understands that feeling strange and out of contact is part of the transference state that describes the patient's reality.

> Ms. H, a new student, had a new patient who initially spoke freely then seemed unable to talk and became silent. An uncomfortable state existed in the room. After a period of this silence, the patient, who liked his own hair, mentioned that the therapist had beautiful hair. Ms. H realized that the patient was referring to himself or to them as one! Voila, the beginning of understanding narcissism!

The Student's Reactions to Supervision

Is the student able to accept and make use of supervision and convey a full picture of the case, or is the student's report an oversimplification or a simple, "I like the patient." Is there a particular style of supervision to which the student best responds? Does the student seem desperate for supervisory interventions, to be told what to do with a patient? How does the student's response to supervision change over time? Underlying much of a student's reaction to supervision is an awareness of one's own primitive impulses and feelings—the countertransference—that is aroused by the patient. The ultimate goal is for the student to demonstrate curiosity about the patient and to share that with the supervisor to enhance understanding of the therapeutic situation.

A student, Ms. T, previously trained as a mental health counselor, was encouraging her patient, who was angry with someone in his residential facility, to talk about his feelings of anger. The patient subsequently began beating up people on the bus and was on the verge of being removed from the program. In supervision, because the student was curious about her patient's reaction, she was helped to explore whether he was being overstimulated in therapy. Her willingness to examine the relationship with her patient led her to wonder if asking about anger resulted in the patient's acting out. She stopped asking him about his feelings and followed the contact function more rigorously. The patient calmed down and stopped acting out on the bus.

THE STUDENT'S INTERACTIONS WITH CLASSMATES

Is the student able to interact with classmates in a flexible, non-defensive manner? How has that relationship changed over time? Are the student's contributions consistently negative or self-aggrandizing, or are they constructive and decidedly geared to help his colleagues?

The same day that Mrs. S was dealing with her rejection of the silent skeleton of a patient, the more experienced class members complimented her on her new and genuine reactions to this patient. The student reacted positively to this peer support because she had wondered whether her reactions to the patient were induced by the patient or were a result of a problem in her personality. The other students' responses and input resolved her resistance to stepping back and considering that her reactions were, indeed, induced by the patient. Instead of her reacting impulsively by, for example, canceling appointments or ending them early, she was eager to learn more about and understand her reactions so she could treat the patient.

In another situation, a female student was the target of verbal aggression from a male student. It was the beginning of the semester, so the

woman could not imagine what she had done to the fellow that might
have offended him—or what was wrong with him that he, without reason, was lashing out at her. In time, instead of repeating her thought pattern, the woman repositioned herself in the class to view and think dif-
ferently about the situation. Instead of focusing on what she might have
done, she considered what might be going on in the classmate's head that
was motivating him to attack her.

The teacher felt that the woman was both aware of and able to manage
her emotional interactions. She did not avoid her antagonist or over-intel-
lectualize the situation but instead began to consider her adversary's
motivations. The teacher concluded that the woman demonstrated both
academic knowledge and understanding and that she was open to learning and was continuing to learn more about herself.

*   *   *

Having presented the above criteria for studying areas of learning for
the student working with the preoedipal patient and the accompanying
vignettes, it might be useful to examine excerpts from a final presentation submitted by a student graduating from fieldwork. Her fieldwork
paper and presentation help illustrate the criteria through a single case
presented by a successful graduate of this introductory clinical level of
training. This student had "gotten it," clearly understanding himself and
his work with the narcissistic patient.

The Graduating Student

The student had selected an externship at a day treatment mental health
center in New York. One of his patients was a 53-year-old self-
described depressed gay female. Ms. T is 50 pounds overweight but
otherwise is relatively well groomed. The patient had been in and out
of community mental health treatment for 17 years.

In **observing the contact function,** the student reported the patient
exhibited apathy toward her, "and the world. From the beginning of our
meetings [the patient] stoically looked out and away from me,
expressed little affect, and provided gossipy information about the program and her life outside [of the treatment facility]. During the beginning and end of each session the patient turned her body so she faced
away from me, stared into space and walked in and out of the room
without any sort of acknowledgement. I have the sense that this psy-

chotic detachment helps her to limit me as an object. It also suggested that I should be cautious not to draw attention to myself."

As for **the student's interventions,** the student concluded, "What was of the utmost importance in developing the narcissistic transference with [the patient] was to limit my contact with her. A flat affect and psychotic detachment made it clear to me that very little stimulation would be tolerated. Ms. T even stated that many relationships had ended because they were too much to handle. So I learned to keep quiet and never look at [the patient]. For the most part, she talked for the entire session."

Occasionally the patient would make contact, which the student/therapist responded to "with a question for consultation." The patient in turn would answer with, "I don't know, what do you think?" "If I responded, she would pause and then start talking about something else, which I took as confirmation that I should not be talking so much. For the most part some joining with the patient, and keeping still and quiet were the key ingredients to developing the narcissistic transference where [the patient] felt at ease enough to talk and not take any action."

After nearly a year of sessions, the student felt she and the patient had "become 'involved'"—a relationship that seemed to grow even closer when the patient actually asked the therapist to intervene in a family matter. Around the same time, one of the student's other patients quit the program and another became ill and was hospitalized, leaving the student with just this one patient—and Ms. T now asked whether she could stay for the extra sessions. "I now felt that Ms. T wanted all of me," the therapist reported.

Recollections of **the student's defenses and her reactions to those defenses** followed. "I tried to explore what the benefits would be, and what would be said in those sessions that have not already been said in the first session, all to limited response. But I was told [by her] on the last go around with this issue that it would be my therapeutic duty to let her stay for three hours so Ms. T could just use the time however she wanted. As she has come to feel that I am all hers and her fantasy has come true, the level of stimulation has increased. Interestingly, I feel more distinct and thought of as an object, but also more threatened."

In reporting these defenses and reactions to those defenses in response to the patient's "psychotic detachment [that] helps her to limit me as an object," the student recalled, "I thought to myself, is this the result of simmering aggression that has to be fended off by removing me as an object? How do I work with a patient when I do not even feel I exist?"

The student indicated that she had learned that in order to work with the severely regressed narcissistic patient "one has to become ego-syntonic with the patient." Using modern psychoanalytic techniques of joining the patient's percepts and metering the stimulation in the room by following the patient's contact function, this student had been able to help the patient develop a narcissistic transference.

Not infrequently, the seven criteria overlap, especially the student's defenses and reactions to those defenses, the student's descriptions of the patient's symbolic and unconscious nonverbal communications, and the student's reactions to the patient and understanding of those reactions.

Acknowledging **the student's descriptions of the patient's symbolic and unconscious nonverbal communications** and **the student's reactions to the patient and understanding of those reactions,** the student wrote, "Throughout this externship I have had feelings of confusion, boredom, indifference and caution with [the patient]. In the beginning of the externship I experienced these feelings as a flaw and attacked myself for being undisciplined and inexperienced, which I have come to understand as my narcissistic defense. However, over time I have begun to perceive these feelings as symbolic communications from the patient, and this has helped in creating an emotionally dynamic experience with [the patient]. I am accepting these powerful feelings not only as just my own but also as the patient's.

"What I came to realize was that by analyzing the narcissistically induced feelings and when appropriately making a joining statement that resonated with these induced feelings, [the patient] became less defensive and was able to talk more about herself and her life rather than to psychically 'leave' the room by talking about others and [mental health center] gossip. Caution and indifference were the first induced feelings that I started to associate with [the patient]. I then had the sense that I was going to be consumed and swallowed up. I was hers for the taking. . . .

"I felt at once loved for being available and symbiotic with [the patient], but also hated because I could not give her everything that she wanted when she wanted it. Being only a part-object, at best, also factored into my feelings of indifference. [The patient] protected herself and me from hostile feelings by denying my existence as well as hers. It seems that this manifested itself through [the patient's] behavior of a rigid posture and looking away as if I did not exist."

Any number of times throughout her presentation, the student acknowledged her **reactions to the patient and her understanding of those reactions.** She noted that the patient gave her "the impression that she is simmering with suppressed rage, and the only way to regulate such rage is to become aloof and withdrawn." The student used the fifty-second session to describe the development of the narcissistic transference and the discharge of negative feelings associated with it. "During this session I was ceremoniously obliterated and emotionally attacked for denying [the patient] the gratification of extra sessions over the previous three weeks."

Once, the patient "let me have it with both barrels," the student recalled, "and I did not counterattack; she and I seemed to both relax. I was relieved to have finally experienced what I had been cautious about for the past year, and I think Ms. T was relieved to have discharged a lot of aggression and rage without me obliterating and rejecting her, as she might have been treated as an infant. By the end of that session, she was talking and engaged in finding me two more patients. And she knew just the right two people. Not only were these sessions pivotal for understanding transference, but they also helped to provide insight into the countertransference feelings I was having with the patient."

Confusion was another induced feeling the student started to recognize as part of the patient's unconscious. The patient would give the therapist "a hodgepodge of information" about the center, "other patients, their problems, and other chatter." During group supervision, the patient was characterized as being like a gossip columnist. In response, the student said she felt like she was "being forced to hear everything written in the *New York Times*," not just the sections or stories that interested her. "It was a force-feeding, just like she may have been force-fed." And when the student read a series of letters, long and detailed, written by the patient, she "felt bewildered with trivial information that diluted the point. It was too much information. I came to think of this process as what might have happened to [the patient]. I was to feel as she did when her mother provided Ms. T with too much bewildering stimulation."

During her supervision, the student found she was not interested in reading the process recording that followed the important fifty-second session. As the supervisor explored her resistance, the student mentioned that she was bored; in turn, the supervisor suggested that her feeling of boredom might be a defense against anger. "After supervision I went back and read the process recording and came to understand that my boredom was a defense against the hatred I had for [the patient] because she acted as if what happened in session 52 did not even exist. How could all those powerful emotions and pivotal moments of that session be completely ignored in the next session? I could not tolerate hating her when she did not hate me at the same time, so I became bored with the session. Coincidentally I was struggling with this very issue in my own analysis. I have been exploring the fear of being hated and hating. Not having a full awareness of all my own feelings keeps me from feeling the emotions of others, which Spotnitz calls counter-transference resistance. Supervision and analysis have been essential in my ability to tolerate feelings that the patient and I have never been able to articulate in words."

The student summed up this relationship and her insights. "Having understood [the patient's] symbolic communications, respected her defenses and joined her emotions, I have been able to provide a good enough environment where [the patient] can talk and feel without act-ing. There have been moments of object transference, but for the most part [the patient] remains in a narcissistic state of objectlessness." Despite this, the patient wanted to continue seeing the therapist, but now at the treatment service, "which I believe to be an attempt at attachment. This primitive attachment is permitting progressive com-munication."

Conclusion

In this paper I have presented some ways to conceptualize success-fully teaching students to work with narcissistic patients and have examined how the teacher, supervisor, and student are able to deter-mine that appropriate learning of how to "be with" the narcissistic patient has occurred. It would seem that in looking back at the seven criteria (student's ability to observe the contact function; student's interventions; student's defenses and reactions to those defenses; stu-dent's descriptions of the patient's symbolic and unconscious verbal and non-verbal communications; student's reactions to the patient and an understanding of those reactions; the student's reaction to supervi-sion; and the student's interactions with classmates) we are determin-ing that the therapist is developing an ability to step back from the reaction to the patient and talk about the experience in an emotion-ally relevant fashion. It may in fact be this ability to be in the moment—to step back and talk about the experience—that is the essential indication that our students and we are more fully under-standing the patient. So when Spotnitz described the goal of treatment as helping the patient to "say everything," he might also be describing the process of psychoanalytic education, where teachers and supervisors help the student "say everything" about the patient with the goal of helping the patient do the same.

REFERENCES

Freud, S. (1914), On narcissism: an introduction. *Standard Edition.* London: Hogarth Press, 14:69–102.

———— (1917), Introductory lectures on psycho-analysis, Part III. *Standard Edition.* London: Hogarth Press, 16:413–447.

———— (1920), Beyond the pleasure principle. *Standard Edition.* London: Hogarth Press, 18:3–64.

———— (1933), New introductory lectures on psycho-analysis. *Standard Edition.* London: Hogarth Press, 22:5–182.

Fleming, J. & S. S. Weiss (1978), Assessment of progress in a training analysis. *The International Review of Psycho-Analysis*, 5:33–43.

Hanigsberg, I. (1978), Philosophy of education in institute training. *Modern Psychoanalysis*, 3:73–81.

Heimann, P. (1968), The evaluation of applicants for psychoanalytic training: the goals of psychoanalytic education and the criteria for the evaluation of applicants. *International Journal of Psychoanalysis*, 49:527–539.

Karon, B. P. (1992), The fear of understanding schizophrenia. *Psychoanalytic Psychology*, 9:191–211.

Kernberg, O. (1975), *Borderline Conditions and Pathological Narcissism.* Northvale, NJ: Jason Aronson.

———— (1986), Institutional problems of psychoanalytic education. *Journal of the American Psychoanalytic Association*, 34:799–834.

———— (1996), Thirty methods to destroy the creativity of psychoanalytic candidates. *International Journal of Psychoanalysis*, 77:1031–1040.

———— (2000a), A concerned critique of psychoanalytic education. *International Journal of Psychoanalysis*, 81:97–120.

———— (2000b), Presidential message. Presentation at the inauguration of the 41st International Psychoanalytical Congress in Santiago, Chile, July 26, 1999. *Bulletin of the International Psychoanalytical Association*, 149:406–407.

Kohut, H. (1971), *The Analysis of the Self.* New York: International Universities Press.

Margolis, D. (1978), Who shall be trained? *Modern Psychoanalysis*, 3:59–72.

Meadow, P. W. (1988), Emotional education: the theory and process of training psychoanalysts. *Modern Psychoanalysis*, 13:209–388.

——— (1991), Resonating with the psychotic patient. *Modern Psychoanalysis*, 16:87–103.

Meadow, P. W. & E. Clevans (1978), A new approach to psychoanalytic teaching. *Modern Psychoanalysis*, 3:29–43.

Pumilia, M. & S. Zaretsky (2004), *Externship Manual for the Paper and Presentation*. The Academy of Clinical and Applied Psychoanalysis. Unpublished.

Rosenfeld, H. (1987), *Impasse and Interpretation: Therapeutic and Antitherapeutic Factors in the Psychoanalytic Treatment of Psychotic, Borderline and Neurotic Patients*. New York: Brunner-Routledge.

Ross, L. (1976), A study of the narcissistic communications of a paranoid patient. *Modern Psychoanalysis*, 2:164–190.

Searles, H. (1965), *Collected Papers on Schizophrenia and Related Subjects*. New York: International Universities Press.

Simenauer, E. (1983), Some aspects of training analysis. *The International Review of Psychoanalysis*, 10:145–157.

Spotnitz, H. (1976a), Trends in modern psychoanalytic supervision. *Modern Psychoanalysis*, 2:201-217.

——— (1976b), Techniques for resolving the narcissistic defense. *Psychotherapy of Preoedipal Conditions*. Northvale, NJ: Jason Aronson.

——— (1976c), Schizophrenia and severe character disorders. *Psychotherapy of Preoedipal Conditions*. Northvale, NJ: Jason Aronson.

——— (1979), Narcissistic countertransference. *Contemporary Psychoanalysis*, 15:545–559.

——— (2004), *Modern Psychoanalysis of the Schizophrenic Patient: Theory of the Technique*. 2004 Second Edition. New York: YBK Publishers.

Stone, L. (1974), The assessment of students' progress. *The Annual of Psychoanalysis*, 2:308–322.

Thoma, H. (1993), Training analysis and psychoanalytic education: proposals for reform. *The Annual of Psychoanalysis*, 21:3–75.

Waelder, R. (1961), The selection of candidates. *International Journal of Psychoanalysis*, 43:283–286.

Wallerstein, R. S. (1978), Perspectives on psychoanalytic training around the world. *International Journal of Psychoanalysis*, 59:477–503.

Weiss, S. S. (1982), The problem of the problem candidate: a significant issue for psychoanalytic educators. *The Annual of Psychoanalysis*, 10:77–92.

Weiss, S. S. & J. Fleming (1975), Evaluation of progress in supervision. *The Psychoanalytic Quarterly*, 44:191–205.

———— (1979), The teaching and learning of the selection process: one aspect of faculty development. *The Annual of Psychoanalysis*, 7:87–109.

Winnicott, D. W. (1975), *Through Paediatrics to Psycho-analysis.* New York: Basic Books.

769 Northfield Ave. LL6
West Orange, NJ 07052
vwsemel@comcast.net

Speaking the Unspeakable

NICOLE KIRMAN

Patients who need to experience the analyst as a good presence, and who succeed in doing so, dread risking the loss of that experience as a consequence of becoming aware of their own anger or any negative feeling toward the analyst. This paper explores the ways in which four patients experienced knowing their feelings of anger toward the analyst. The author discusses the narcissistic transference and the narcissistic defense and explains how two of these patients were gradually able to move from a narcissistic transference to an object transference.

Modern analysis has from the beginning focused on the impact that mismanagement of aggression can have on the psyche. While some people exhibit excessive or uncontrolled outwardly directed aggression, others direct their aggression inwards. Spotnitz (1976, 2004) has written in detail about how essential it is for the analyst to deal with this issue, which presents itself in analysis as negative transference and negative transference resistance. Modern analysts have elaborated in their writings the various forms that negative transferences can take and the multitudinous ways that resistances to feeling and expressing the negative transference in verbally appropriate ways can manifest themselves.

This paper will take a closer look at a form of the resistance that some patients exhibit, one which tends to be glossed over, perhaps because it seems so obvious. Patients who tend to direct their aggression toward themselves and who are very self-critical and self-attacking, avoid experiencing and expressing negative transference feelings for a variety of reasons. A common motivation for such resistance is the fear of retaliation from the analyst. Modern psychoanalysis has empha-

© 2004 CMPS/*Modern Psychoanalysis*, Vol. 29, No. 2

sized the importance of the patient's fear that his own aggression may destroy the needed analyst (the resistance of object protection). A more subtle form of this kind of resistance, which I will focus on, relates to the nature of the patient's connection with the object. That is, patients who need to experience the analyst as a good presence, and who succeed in doing so, dread risking the loss of that experience as a consequence of experiencing their own anger or any negative feeling toward the analyst. Any such negative feeling threatens to break the positive connection with the analyst because the patient's anger drives out the internal image of the analyst from the patient's psyche, leaving the patient bereft, alone, and lost.

Several patients whom I have treated exhibited a fairly common defense against knowing their aggressive feelings—they seemed stuck in the status quo resistance of a positive narcissistic transference. However, when they were later able to "say whatever came to their mind," these patients gave similar accounts of their feelings. One must keep in mind that these patients were able to verbalize and give a description and an explanation of their experience once they had resolved the resistance connected with it. In other words, while they were living the defense, they were unaware of it and had no words for it. All they could do was to act it out.

Case Vignette: Mrs. D

Mrs. D is a particularly good illustration of this phenomenon because she recapitulated in a few years, i.e., a relatively short time, and in a clear fashion the various stages of the narcissistic transference. Mrs. D came to see me after a tragic event tore her life apart and threw her into a deep depression in which she felt at times self-destructive and even suicidal. She could barely function on an everyday basis, and her sessions became the only place where she could talk about her feelings and her concerns. With the rest of the world, she felt she had to conceal her despair, behave as if nothing had happened, and work on coping and functioning. But mostly, for the first time in her life, she found herself at the mercy of feelings that she had been able to ignore or deny all her life.

Through the analysis, Mrs. D discovered that she could hate, despair, wish to hurt or kill, and have a host of feelings which had been forbidden to her. She also discovered her great need for connection. Because the analytic couch was the only place where she could express all her pain and confusion, the analytic office became a valuable place.

At first, Mrs. D regressed to a period of objectlessness: I felt that I did not exist or rather that I was on par with the walls, the windows, and the couch. I was an integral part of the place where she could pour out her pain and process all the bad feelings she was experiencing since everywhere else she had to hide. I accepted my place. Her only contact with me was to ask how long she had to suffer like this.

After some time, Mrs. D's transference became very intense. Eventually, our sessions became the most important thing in her life. At the height of the narcissistic transference, we were so well attuned to each other that when she contacted me, it seemed as though I always came up with the exactly right answer or response, and she would take in my words as if they were delicious food.

Mrs. D not only took in my words, but she also took me in as an idealized image. She carried me with her in a strong symbiosis. She described her experience in this way: At night, before she fell asleep, my image would come to her, and she could gauge the connection she had with me at that moment by the position in which she found me in her room. When she felt closest to me, I was right near her, near her face. Or when she experienced some disappointment in me, I would end up in a far corner of her room. This image would come up spontaneously and she felt that she had no control over it: She could not move me to a different location more in tune with her conscious wishes.

Mrs. D oscillated between times when she wanted to be alone and times when not being connected was totally painful and despairing. She wanted to be alone because any contact with another felt like an imposition—she could not be herself or do what she wanted; she felt impelled to become totally subservient to the needs and wishes of the other. On the other hand, there were times when being alone became terrifying.

In analysis, she discovered that she could contact me by phone when the isolation became unbearable to her, i.e., when the "demons" would invade her and she had impulses to self-mutilate. She felt terrified and would call my number, but she revealed later that often she did not want me to answer the telephone—she just wanted to hear my voice on the answering machine. The contact then was very controlled and minimal. A contact with a real object would have been too threatening to her fragile ego; the confrontation of "another," too much. The sound of my voice was reassuring without being a threat. Now—several years later—when she calls me up, she seems to have a radar as to when she can find me: she calls when a patient has just left or when I have just walked into my office or just before I leave the office—just in time to get me.

This happy state went on for several years, during which Mrs. D was reconstituting herself, becoming aware and accepting of her destructive impulses, getting familiar with her "demons," coming up with memories, and getting psychically stronger. Eventually, I lost some of my perfection and she started making mild recriminations until one session in which I did the "wrong" thing. She experienced an intervention of mine as my pushing her to grow up. My intervention was ill-timed, or so it seemed.

At the next session, Mrs. D declared:

> I am feeling like I've resolved something, like I've moved on and feel much better. I realized that I am no longer angry with you. You are back—not too close but back. . . . I don't like it [i.e., to be angry at you] at all. It feels very uncomfortable, terrible. When I am angry, I feel like I have done something wrong, something terribly wrong, like a sin. It feels like something not allowed in this world. So I end up turning things around against myself. I end up wrong.

This is a beautiful illustration of the narcissistic defense, where the anger is experienced as so bad and dangerous that it is turned against the self. The patient went on to say, "I also end up feeling disconnected. I can't get any comfort. I end up disconnected, alone, isolated. It feels intolerable."

A few sessions later, she added:

> I feel I'm fighting a battle. I am feeling very angry. I am angry and I have the feeling that you left me, and the flood of being lost and disconnected . . . I don't know which way to go. . . . There is some severing that anger triggers—it is so powerful, it breaks all connection.

Case Vignette: Mrs. R

This "severing triggered by anger" seems to be the same phenomenon described by Mrs. R, a shy, retiring woman who had difficulty saying anything when she began what turned out to be a long-term analysis. She began her analysis because of a profound depression although she was able to function in a restricted way. Eventually she was able to talk and developed a strong narcissistic transference. Even though over the years she was able to grow and become somewhat more assertive, her attitude towards me did not change: she had only positive feelings. Whenever she became quiet during a session, I suspected that some negative reaction had occurred. When occasionally the possibility of some negativity was explored, she denied having any. Finally, after many years of treatment, I said something that got her very upset and angry, as I later found out. During this session Mrs. R said nothing that revealed her state of mind. She was quiet to the end of the session—which ended soon after my upsetting remark. That was not very unusual for this patient. It was at the next session that she revealed her reaction and explained what she had experienced: when, at the previous session, I said something that angered her (neither of us can now remember what I said), she felt herself shutting down and becoming cold. She sensed suddenly a great distance between us. But it was only after she left the office that she realized that she was very angry. She also realized that I no longer meant anything to her—I, who knew her intimately, whom she always carried with her in her mind, whom she felt she could always turn to for emotional help, who had been so patient with her, and towards whom she had felt such gratitude. She suddenly felt totally disconnected from me. She had thrown me out of her emotional awareness. As she put it, " It felt as if I had ejected you from my mind. Instead of a constant presence who accompanied me everywhere, there was nothing, a void." She had banished me from her mind; she also considered banishing me from her life by ending the analytic relationship right then and there. But she refrained from acting on that impulse.

Discussion

In this case, as with Mrs. D, the anger had the impact of severing the affective bond. Both patients were in a comfortable narcissistic transference when the analyst made the dystonic intervention that provoked the anger and interrupted the blissful state. One can be assured that this was not the first time that this analyst made some intervention that could have been experienced as dystonic by those patients, but it was the first time that each patient allowed herself the reaction of anger and its full consequences. This would indicate some readiness on the part of these patients to experience these feelings.

If one considers the mechanism that is triggered by these patients' anger, it does not appear to be a question of the good object turning into a bad object. Rather it seems to be a good object or no object at all, i.e., a complete withdrawal of cathexis. However, this does not seem to be the same mechanism as the psychotic's withdrawal and disconnection— here the patient feels all alone, as in a void, with a limited amount of energy cathexis available. But the psyche is not attacked since there is no disintegration or disconnection with reality. Rather, it is diminished and there is a sense of loss and of being lost because, by losing the internal image, the patient has lost a part of herself, a part of her ego.

What seems to be severed is the primitive bond which originally linked the baby to the mother and that is now relived in the narcissistic transfer-ence. Spotnitz and Meadow (1976) describe this powerful connection:

> The psyche of the preverbal patient contains a strong libidinal attachment to others and a strong desire for the warmth and closeness that others can provide. This is the kind of closeness one expects during the first year of life—to be held, to be walked, to be rocked, to be talked to, and in gen-eral to be soothed. It is these longings that are reactivated in the narcis-sistic transference. (p. 73)

Mrs. D had taken in the analyst as a part of herself, a good part, a good object—therefore Mrs. D was also good. But her goodness depended on the reflection of the good-analyst image. The connection, the bond with the good object, also felt like a lifeline. It offered com-fort and security and protected the patient from being prey to terrifying anxieties. With this connection, she felt able to grow. Without it, the patient was "alone" and "disconnected," a condition that felt intolerable to the dependent ego.

When that narcissistic break occurs—and there is usually a point in the analysis where it does occur—when the patient experiences some misunderstanding on the part of the analyst, there are several possible consequences: 1) The patient finds the injury too great and irreparable and leaves the analyst; 2) The patient engages in object protection through self-attack, rationalization, or some other means in order to maintain the positive transference; or 3) The patient is strong enough to have it out with the analyst and to go on with the analysis.

Case Vignette: Ms. P

Ms. P is an excellent illustration of the first possibility—someone who, having felt "abandoned" by her previous analyst in a time of crisis, acted out on her destructive impulse and left her. In looking back on that break, she does not talk about cutting off her analyst from her mind field, probably because acting it out took the place of the feeling. But reflecting on this event several years later and with that much more analysis, she surmised:

> It was a matter of, she wasn't the person I thought she was—and I needed her to be that person still, even if it meant I didn't continue. Better to be the person I thought she was, who failed me terribly, than just another flawed person who was just muddling along.

Ms. P was in a regressed state and could not tolerate the feelings aroused in a relationship with a separate object—such as the feelings of disappointment. Nor could she consider that such feelings are inevitable in a relationship. This patient left the analyst to maintain the hope that she would find an object who would never give her those feelings. Ms. P was in a narcissistic transference with an omnipotent analyst, and she needed that state maintained for a longer period of time before she could tolerate acknowledging the failings of her analyst. She would rather leave the (external) analyst and the analysis than alter her internal image of that analyst's omnipotence and omniscience, an image that she could not give up at that time.

Case Vignette: Ms. A

A fourth patient, Ms. A, is an example of the second possibility, of someone who avoids experiencing aggression toward the analyst in order to preserve the relationship. Ms. A has been in treatment with me for a long time. She originally came to my office as a depressed, suicidal, impulse-ridden young woman who was filled with bitterness and rage. Over the years, she frequently acted out her negative feelings but eventually learned to express some of them in words. Recently, she revealed that right now she does not want to have any negative feelings toward me because when she senses them, she sees herself "floating off into space without a tether" or just "lost in space." She also does not seem to be aware that her anger is cutting off any connection to me, but only of its result—her feelings of disconnection and their consequences, that she is lost in space. For this patient, at this time, her connection to me keeps her grounded on this earth.

Discussion

In both these cases, the consequence of having and feeling the anger toward the analyst is a premature interruption of merging with the object that the narcissistic transference allowed them. These patients use whatever tools they have at their disposal to protect the internal image and maintain the affective bond. And it is the role of the modern analyst to help them maintain it until they are ready to discard it.

During this state of narcissistic transference, as Goldberg (1995) described it, it is as though the patient were "in a warm bath . . . so that there is not so much difference between what is his/her body and what is outside" (p. 80). These last two patients were not yet ready to move on to a more object-related stage in the analysis. They needed more time to grow up, which the narcissistic transference afforded them.

However, the first two patients (Mrs. D and Mrs. R), as it turned out, exemplified the third possibility. They were ready to leave the merged narcissistic state and enter the object world. For them, ejecting the internalized analyst impression became a first step toward differentiation and individuation.

Even this first step evolved over a period of time. The sessions following the one in which Mrs. D had the experience of disconnection with me were filled with reactions to this event, in which she went back and forth, feeling angry with me and not feeling angry, feeling disconnected and feeling reconnected. She was obviously working through the impact of the intervention:

> Talking about frustration . . . I feel disconnected . . . but it does not feel bad. I just have not thought about you. I used to think of you every night before I went to sleep. I am not doing that anymore. And last night was Sunday night [*that was when her need for contact became most intense and frightening*]. I did not even notice it. It is as though I am feeling independent, like a child who suddenly does not need her mother. I am aware of having gone through several different stages with you.

Her increasing individuation was also manifested in increased desires for object relatedness and dissatisfaction with the limitations of the analytic relationship. At various times, she told me:

P: The frustration comes from the fact that you are not answering my question, you are not gratifying me.

A: What should I be saying?

P: You won't say that I've worked hard and done a great job and that I am doing well. I seem to need your approval or confirmation. Why? Why? I have just changed what I want to hear from you. It's no longer what it was two minutes ago. What I want to hear—I can't say it—it's too humiliating; my mind won't allow it. What I want to hear from you is that you love me and that I am special.

Mrs. D is clearly now relating to me as a separate object, another individual from whom she wants something, some love and recognition. In fact, immediately after putting her request into words, she became like an adolescent giving up the original object to find in the world her own appropriate object: She remembers feeling special when she first met her husband. She then realizes that she wants to feel that again. She wants someone to go on vacation with, to have dinner with, to have sex with. This is the first time that she has seriously considered the possibility of wanting another partner. She is giving me up—this frustrating, ungratifying object—for the potentiality of real gratification.

A similar progression occurred with Mrs. R after the session in which her anger at me severed her connection with me. As she later related, she postponed the decision whether to stay in analysis or quit. As the time of the following session neared, Mrs. R was feeling "strangely strong" and "independent," so she decided to come to the session and have it out with me. During the session, as she herself explained, I had a sense that Mrs. R did feel stronger because she spoke with feeling and with confidence. She also agreed to go on with the analysis. A few sessions later, she revealed that she had accepted my shortcomings and was on her way to forgiving me, and that I was back in her mind but in a different way: not so essentially needed. She also revealed that she did not feel depressed—which was not uncommon since she did have periods of time when she was not depressed—but, and this was more unusual, she did not feel self-critical. This she experienced as a real change.

A couple of months later, Mrs. R reported another change that she attributed to this event. All her life, she had felt inhibited in her actions. She did not feel free to do anything without the permission or the encouragement of someone. It was not that she was not capable of doing it, just that she experienced a holding back, a brake on all her impulses so that she could only do what was "okayed by someone else." But now, she felt that this inhibition had disappeared; she could be an agent of her own will. She was elated by this development and was convinced that this release of the inhibition was irreversible. In this case, in order to have all her feelings, including her feelings of anger, Mrs. R had to tolerate the isolation it forced her to experience. This resulted in some major character changes for Mrs. R: it provided the final blow to her depression by relieving her of some self-critical tendencies, and it lifted her inhibition permanently.

By allowing themselves the anger, even though it meant ejecting the analyst from their minds and remaining alone, at least temporarily, both Mrs. D and Mrs. R have accomplished an important step forward toward maturation and object relationship. In some ways it is the task of every human being who, in order to grow up, individuate, and stand on one's own two feet, must be willing to tolerate the loss of narcissistic bonds and accept the otherness of any object. In analysis, this entails moving from a narcissistic transference to an object transference—which does not mean that regression to narcissistic transference will not happen again. The patient will keep shifting back and forth between the two transferences until object relatedness is securely attained.

Narcissistic Transference

What these four patients have in common is that they were all in a narcissistic transference in which they experienced the analyst as undifferentiated from them and part of themselves. This corresponds to a preverbal stage of the infant's psychic development in which the infant does not distinguish between self and object and there is no clear division between them. As Margolis (1981) described it:

> In keeping with the confusion between self and object images that the patient has retained from his early narcissistic period, the significance he attaches to the analyst is now evidenced by a similar confusion in the patient's perception of himself and the analyst. (p. 173)

The modern analyst encourages this regression so that the patient can relive in the present the preoedipal fixations and conflicts and, this time around, put the conflicts into words. This allows the patient to develop and grow, whether the transference is positive or negative. As modern analysts, we take into account the importance of bringing out the negative transference [cf. Spotnitz (1976, 2004), Epstein (1999), Kirman (1986), Liegner (1980), Meadow(1996)] and that is indeed what was in the analyst's mind in three of the four cases presented (in the case of Ms. P, the break was circumstantial rather than intentional).

Perhaps what has not been stressed enough is the powerful impact of the positive narcissistic transference. In that transferential state of merger, the patient projects onto the analyst whatever characteristic he/she needs in order to grow and reincorporates whatever is needed from the analyst for that growth. As Spotnitz and Meadow (1976) put it: "The syntonic feeling of oneness is a curative one, while the feeling of aloneness, the withdrawn state, is merely protective" (p. 67).

However, the positive narcissistic transference and the bond that gets established between the patient and the analyst can become itself a source of pleasure difficult to give up. Spotnitz and Meadow explain:

> When a positive narcissistic attachment has been formed, we have seen that the patient seeks the analyst's approval, and only with great difficulty relinquishes the enjoyment of a positive attachment. This period precedes a clear demarcation between self and primary object—the good feelings come from symbiosis with a powerful figure.

Margolis (1981) also sees this pleasure as the source of a status quo resistance:

> The peak of this form of resistance is reached in the *status quo* resistance, when the merged narcissistic transference has attained full development and the patient experiences a comfortable sense of unity with the object (the analyst), which he strives to sustain unaltered forever after. (p. 181)

Since the narcissistic transference can be such a pleasurable state of affairs, patients often, in order to move out of the narcissistic transference to a more object-oriented transference, require a jarring, dystonic experience with the analyst. This is indeed what happened with the first two patients, Mrs. D and Mrs. R.

However, the other two patients, Ms. P and Ms. A, found ways to avoid leaving the narcissistic transference. As we saw above, there is another reason, in addition to its pleasure, why it is so difficult for some patients to give up the narcissistic transference. For the patient who is more regressed and whose ego is weaker, giving up the symbiotic connection is intolerable. Like the infant who cannot live without the care and support of the mother, this patient experiences the loss of the analyst as threatening, unbearable anxiety. It also represents the impoverishment of his ego. A part of himself, the part that he introjected from the analyst, is also ejected from his mind field.

Narcissistic Defense

Another thing that these patients have in common is that they all started with a powerful narcissistic defense, that is, in order to protect the object from their destructive impulses, they would rather attack themselves or their mind or act out self-destructively. The narcissistic defense comes into action because unconsciously:

1. the object is felt as too desperately essential to the individual—its loss would entail feelings of helplessness, dependency, and unbearable anxiety. The patient's fear of disconnection seems to go beyond "separation anxiety," or is a very primitive form of it, because it points to a loss of a lifeline. The individual is faced with total isolation and aloneness, a situation which is experienced as utterly intolerable;
2. the negative, aggressive feelings are felt as too dangerous because they threaten that relationship. For these patients, anger, perhaps because it is so strong, perhaps because it has been repressed for so long and has thereby increased so much, can only be experienced as totally noxious and deadly.

In any case, when the anger is allowed to rise to the surface, it must eliminate, eject, kill off the object.

It must be emphasized that the object that is being protected is the internal object. As Mrs. D put it: "You are my creation. I have created you. Who you really are, I don't know and don't want to know. You're in my mind when I want you."

Both Ms. A, who made it clear that she did not want to have any negative feelings, and Ms. P, who left the analyst, are still struggling under the influence of the narcissistic defense. Ironically, they acted out this defense in totally opposite fashions: Ms. A by maintaining her relationship with her analyst at her own expense, and Ms. P by ending her relationship.

It may seem paradoxical to say that Ms. P preserved her connection to the object by leaving her, but not if one makes the distinction between the internal and the external object. Ms. P sacrificed her relationship with the external object—the analyst—in order to preserve the internal object as she needed her to be. She left the analyst partly as an act of revenge, but mostly to maintain the wished-for omnipotence of this analyst. Many patients in a preoedipal regression would rather believe that the analyst refuses for some unknown reason to use his or her omniscience and omnipotence on the patient's behalf than to believe that the analyst is after all a limited human being—with feet of clay.

Despite their needs to maintain the narcissistic connection, both Ms. P and Ms. A are wrestling with aggressive impulses toward that object. In the case of Ms. P, some destructive impulse was acted out and the analytic relationship was ended. However, Ms. P has stated that she always kept in the back of her mind the thought and wish that some day she would be able to go back to her old analyst and reconcile—which indicates that some libidinal connection was maintained even after the break.

In the case of Ms. A, one can surmise that her destructive impulses still feel too powerful to control or that her ego is still too weak. As a result, she is afraid to get near a situation that would provoke those impulses and is forced to resort to the narcissistic defense in order to protect her connection to the analyst. It is to the detriment of the patient insofar as she is unconsciously putting restrictions on what she can or cannot access in her personality.

In contrast, the first two patients described, Mrs. D and Mrs. R, illustrate what happens when a patient gives up the narcissistic defense. Much work has taken place to resolve the resistance and to prepare the patient for that achievement. And, as with any psychic change, it does not happen suddenly, nor does it emerge in its final form; there is regression and progression over a period of time, a back-and-forth movement, as the change is integrated into the character.

However, both these patients enable us to observe that moment when the individual gives up the narcissistic defense, when some aggression is released and turned toward the analyst. Before the feeling of anger itself can be experienced, the aggressive impulse has had its impact: the internal imago of the analyst has been annihilated, wiped out, expelled from the mind field of the patient, and the emotional connection to the analyst has been severed. The patient is on his or her own. The unconscious impulse that lies behind the ejection of the analyst imago is clearly the wish to destroy. The analyst has been killed off.

Because, unlike Ms. P and Ms. A, both these patients experienced this state of affairs as painful but not intolerable, they were able to process the event, eventually to feel the anger and yet go back to the analyst and speak what had been unspeakable; that is, put into words to this object the negative feelings and thoughts they were harboring at the moment. As a result, the relationship was renewed, but on a different footing. Both patients talked of a greater independence from the analyst and a recognition that the analyst might be different from them. They had entered the world of object relationship.

For both Mrs. D and Mrs. R this represented a great leap forward. They were relieved of their depression, liberated from some of their inhibitions, and were becoming interested in obtaining from the world gratifications which the analyst could not provide. For them, the phenomenon that led to the expelling of the analyst imago from their psychic life had very positive outcomes.

REFERENCES

Epstein, L. (1999), The analyst's "bad-analyst feelings": a counterpart to the process of resolving implosive defenses. *Contemporary Psychoanalysis*, 35:311–325.

Goldberg, J. (1995), Psychoanalyzing the body. *Modern Psychoanalysis*, 20:79–90.

Kirman, J. (1986), The management of aggression in modern psychoanalytic treatment. *Modern Psychoanalysis*, 11:37–49.

Liegner, E. (1980), The hate that cures: the psychological reversibility of schizophrenia. *Modern Psychoanalysis*, 5:5–95.

Meadow, P. W. (1996), Negative union. *Modern Psychoanalysis*, 21:293–303.

Margolis, B. (1981), Narcissistic transference: further considerations. *Modern Psychoanalysis*, 6:171–182.

Spotnitz, H. (1976), *Psychotherapy of Preoedipal Conditions*. New York: Jason Aronson.

——— (2004), *Modern Psychoanalysis of the Schizophrenic Patient*. 2004 Second Edition. New York: YBK Publishers.

Spotnitz, H. & P. W. Meadow (1976), *Treatment of the Narcissistic Neuroses*. New York: The Manhattan Center for Advanced Psychoanalytic Studies.

254 East 68th Street
New York, N.Y. 10021
nkirman@earthlink.net

Publish or Perish: Writing Blocks in Dissertation Writers—The ABD Impasse

ROSE FICHERA McALOON

This paper explores the internal conflicts that may derail efforts to undertake or complete a dissertation. In the review of literature on this subject and in several illuminating case studies, the author focuses on four indicators: fantasy of the meaning and significance of doctoral dissertation; evidence of drive fusion or defusion; sexual identity and object choice difficulties; and potential for drive satisfaction. Preliminary findings are proposed and topics for further research are suggested.

Publish or perish. This dictum strikes fear in the hearts of many graduate students. "ABD," "All But Dissertation," is the acronym for the unfinished, *manqué* state applied to candidates who have completed all the requirements for the doctoral degree except the final research project. For "ABDs" this maxim can be reframed into "Finish or Perish." I have come to see the ABD designation as a kind of special status—an incomplete, deficient state of "perpetual becoming," not of "being," a condition unconsciously used to torment the self and others, characterized by unrealized promise and a dogged inability or unwillingness to complete this final academic hurdle.

This is a state I know well and which I have been studying for the past fifteen years in my work with psychoanalytic candidates and graduate students. These students come from various disciplines and are for the most part enrolled at prestigious universities. They enter treatment because they

© 2004 CMPS/*Modern Psychoanalysis*, Vol. 29, No. 2

are unable to complete what they have come to regard as the crowning achievement of their academic careers, the doctoral dissertation. By the time many of them reach my office, they are in a state of despair—frustrated, humiliated, and hopeless. Up to now most have performed consistently well in school and have derived a large measure of their self-esteem from their academic achievements. Their feelings of helplessness puzzle and frighten them. They come in response to a flyer posted in their university libraries offering help with dissertation-writing impasses or because a friend or one of my colleagues has sent them. In the initial interview I ask what it was about the flyer that caught their attention, and they respond invariably that they would like to make progress on their projects and would like to stop torturing and isolating themselves.

Theoretical Considerations: The Etiology of Writing Blocks

In the literature review that follows I will sample the literature on writing blocks and illustrate aspects of these theoretical formulations with case material. Persons working in other disciplines, such as psychology and education, have written about this topic, but in this paper, I will limit myself to sampling the psychoanalytic literature, and I will touch upon Meadow's (2003) thoughts about blocks to experiencing pleasure. Although much of this literature discusses writing inhibitions experienced by creative artists, I believe the conflicts and dynamics presented below are applicable to dissertators as well. The blank page arouses terror in both graduate students and novelists, and formulating, crafting, and executing a dissertation to completion can be as painful as creating the universe of a novel. Words are the currency in both endeavors, and their sequencing and accumulation can be accomplished at a tortured snail's pace or with lightening speed. When thoughts are expressed in words and make their way onto the page in a timely fashion, we say we are productive, but when our ideas fail to appear on the page, we say we are blocked. It is the origin and function of this blockage that this literature review will describe.

Sigmund Freud: Eros and Thanatos

Freud, who wrote prolifically and without apparent difficulty, initially formulated writing disturbances as "inhibitions" originating from unresolved conflicts between two equally powerful forces. Although he wrote little about writing blocks specifically, he did write at length about sources of inspiration for authors and artists such as Shakespeare (Freud, 1913) and Leonardo da Vinci (Freud, 1911). In "The Paths to the Formation of Symptoms" the twenty-third of his *Introductory Lectures on Psychoanalysis* (1916–17), he draws comparisons between dreams, daydreams, symptoms, fantasies, and art and views impediments to creativity as a struggle between the demands of the pleasure and reality principles. He regarded artistic endeavors as expressions of ungratified fantasies, a view literary critics (Crews, 1975) labeled "reductionistic," and which psychoanalytic theorists such as Rank (1929, 1932), Klein (1975), Segal (1952), and McDougall (1989, 1991) reframed and amplified. Especially disturbing to his critics is Freud's (1916–17) characterization of creative efforts as neurotic and the artist as someone who desires to win honor, power, wealth, fame, and the love of women, but

> lacks the means of achieving these satisfactions. Consequently, like any other unsatisfied man, he turns away from reality and transfers all his interest, and his libido too, to the wishful constructions of his life of phantasy. (p. 376)

Despite criticism from feminists and those who denounce Freud's formulation of the creative process as "pathological," I find it useful. It describes a mental state common to all the cases discussed, all of whom are women and whose fantasies about the meaning and possible outcome of the project impeded progress to completion.

For Freud, inspiration originated from unresolved oedipal conflicts, the resolution of which is the developmental imperative of every individual. This struggle between desire and prohibition, Laplanche and Pontalis (1973) remind us, is not reducible to the "actual influence exerted by the parental couple over the child," but rather to the broader "prohibition against incest which bars the way to naturally sought satisfaction and forms an indivisible link between wish and law." It is these "three points of the triangle" rather than "any particular parental image" that "are destined to be internalized and survive in the structure of the personality" (pp. 285–286).

Thus we see that impediments to "naturally sought satisfaction" were initially linked in Freud's mind to the incest taboo. These repressive mechanisms block the writer from expressing powerful forbidden wishes and the act of writing becomes a dangerous transgression arousing crippling castration anxiety and suffering, theorized by Freud as pleasure perverted. In "Inhibitions, Symptoms and Anxiety," (1926) Freud claims that Eros is responsible for blockages to writing:

> Analysis shows that when activities such as . . . writing . . . are subjected to neurotic inhibitions it is because the physical organs brought into play—the fingers . . . have become too strongly eroticized. . . . As soon as writing, which entails making a liquid flow out of a tube on to a piece of white paper, assumes the significance of copulation . . . writing [is] stopped because [it] represents the performance of a forbidden sexual act. (pp. 89–90)

However, in 1920, with the publication of "Beyond the Pleasure Principle," Freud introduced a radically different source of inhibition, the death instinct. In "The Two Classes of Instincts" Freud (1923) formulated the concept of a death drive, or Thanatos, difficult to discern and observable primarily through its derivative, sadism:

> According to this view we have to distinguish two classes of instincts, one of which, the sexual instincts of Eros, is by far the more conspicuous and accessible to study. It comprises not merely the uninhibited sexual instinct proper and the instinctual impulses of an aim-inhibited or sublimated nature derived from it, but also the self-preservative instinct, which must be assigned to the ego. . . . That second class of instincts was not so easy to point to; in the end we came to recognize sadism as its representative. On the basis of theoretical considerations, supported by biology, we put forward the hypothesis of a death instinct, the task of which is to lead organic life back into the inanimate state. (p. 40)

As part of this new formulation, Freud introduced the idea of drive fusion, a concept that he found difficult to explain, but which in time became central to his new construct. "From this point on," write Laplanche and Pontalis (1973), "the destructive tendencies are accorded the same force as sexuality; the two face each other on the same ground, and they are met in behavior (sado-masochism), psychical agencies (super-ego), and types of object relations that are accessible to psychoanalytic investigation" (p. 180). However, it must be noted that Freud did not assign equal status to the drives. Drive defusion, that is, energy not bound by libido, now signaled the successful splitting of Thanatos from Eros. In the defused drive state, the potential for destructive action can often overpower the desire to create.

In "Dostoevsky and Parricide" Freud (1928) posits a new source of writing inhibition, the need for self-punishment. A compulsive gambler,

Dostoevsky was able to write only when destitute. It was only "when his sense of guilt was satisfied by the punishments he had inflicted on himself," says Freud, that the "the inhibition upon his work became less severe and he allowed himself to take a few steps along the road to success" (p. 191). The rest of the time, the author's harsh superego prohibited him from pursuing his art. Loosening the stranglehold of this critical function became for Freud the goal of treatment.

Otto Rank: The Birth Trauma and Individuation

Rank, cited by Freud in the "Two Classes of Instincts" as providing good examples of the existence of defused energy in neurotic acts of revenge, later broke with his mentor and went on to write extensively about artistic creation and the nature of blockage. Himself a failed artist, Rank's interest in the creative process led him to treat many writers, Anais Nin among them. For Rank (1929), the struggle between the forces of life and death began with the "birth trauma," the source of human anxiety, not the oedipal conflict as posited by Freud. Birth, "the primal castration," was the "separation of the child from the mother," and the quest for pleasure specifically had as its aim, according to Rank, "the re-establishment of the intrauterine primal pleasure" (pp.17–18). The birth experience is, then, not only a triumph of the will, but also the beginning of a life of struggle, ultimately against death. In this formulation, conflicts originate from ambivalence stemming from this first act of separation and bring about a lifelong struggle between being known and remaining hidden.

In *Art and Artist*, Rank (1932) argues that the artist must find a balance between two contradictory impulses: the simultaneous wish for and fear of separation. Both "creature" and "creator," the writer must also differentiate himself from existing forms and ideologies if individuation and originality are to be achieved. And yet this struggle for emancipation has imbedded in it the countervailing desire for "the potential restoration of a union with the Cosmos, which once existed and then was lost" (p. 67). Blockage, then, is caused by an inability to negotiate between these two conflicting drives and overcome only through an act of *will*, a deliberate and powerful assertion of the ego. It is this heroic affirmation that makes creative expression and sublimation possible. Inhibitions to writing are simply the ego's way of protecting itself against the fear and guilt of asserting one's uniqueness and individuality (p. 387).

Melanie Klein and Hannah Segal: Envy, Guilt, and Reparation

Klein (1975) focused her work on the preverbal fantasies of rage and aggression in children, an interest she links to Freud's death instinct theory, a theory she utilizes more extensively than many classical Freudians. In Klein's formulation it is the infant's innate ambivalence toward incorporating the mother's breast that causes it to project its own innate aggression outward. Ego development then is a continual series of introjections and projections of part-objects and later whole objects.

In Kleinian theory, working through the depressive position, the stage in which the infant must accept the fact that the breast is both good and bad, the object of both love and hate, is the developmental milestone equivalent to the resolution of the oedipal conflict. Envy of the power and creative potential of the symbolic breast arouse guilt, a feeling that can be expiated only through acts of reparation. For Klein and her followers, the wish for reparation is the primary motive of creative endeavors. In this formulation, writing becomes a way of confronting conflicts rather than evading or deflecting them.

Klein never wrote about blockage directly, but her ideas were broadly applied to the problem by her followers. Hannah Segal, a disciple who popularized many of Klein's views, wrote extensively about creativity and aesthetics. Inhibitions to artistic endeavors originated from an inability to overcome depressive anxiety. More interesting for our purposes is Segal's (1955) account of a blocked writer for whom the act of writing became an act of aggression. The realization that words had become weapons of "chopping" and "cutting" forced this patient to confront her own destructiveness, her fear of object loss, and her terror of death. Not writing, then, became a way of magically controlling and avoiding death. Through the transference the patient was then able to work through the paranoid-schizoid position back into and through the depressive position and finally to mourn the loss of the internal figure now represented by the analyst. Ultimately it was through writing that true individuation was achieved (p. 295).

Joyce McDougall: Trauma and Sexual Identity Disturbances

McDougall (1989) builds on Segal's formulations but broadens the parameters of the discussion to include a sexual identity component and argues that, in fact, many patients "seek psychoanalytic help not for their sexual acts and object-choices but because of blockage in their professional activities" (p. 218). In "The Dead Father: On Early Psychic Trauma and its Relation to Disturbances in Sexual Identity and in Creative Activity," McDougall (1989) investigates the vicissitudes of the creative process and of the "complex internal drama" (p. 207) that produces inhibitions to work in the case of Benedicte, a novelist on the cusp of achieving success.

Benedicte entered treatment because of a debilitating fear of turning 40, her father's age when he died, and because she was completely blocked in her writing. In the first session she revealed haltingly that her father had died when she was fifteen months old, that her mother had kept this information from her, telling her that he was ill, and that at the age of five a neighbor had finally told her the truth. Subsequently her mother had felt so uncomfortable with her widowed status that she never spoke to her daughter about her father and instead put all her energy into trying to replace him. And when she found the manuscript of an opera labored over by her then adolescent daughter, she destroyed it. Benedicte, who was a lesbian, abhorred her mother's "femininity" (and surely her mother's destructive action) and yet the two women with whom she was involved were both widows with children. This left her with an internal world, argues McDougall (1989), populated only by a distant (and hostile) mother and a shadow father. This deficit made it impossible for her to integrate aspects of her feminine and masculine self:

> Reflection has led me to the conviction that the creative process depends to a considerable extent on the integration of bisexual drives and fantasies. Our intellectual and artistic creations are, so to speak, parthenogenetically created children. A breakdown in the capacity to work creatively frequently involves an interdiction concerning unconscious homosexual identifications, as well as unresolved conflicts attached to the significant inner objects involved. . . . An unconscious refusal to become aware of and explore one's capacity for ambisexual identifications may well involve the risk of producing writer's block. (p. 209)

In this paper, McDougall also writes about the special meaning words come to assume for blocked writers. Words, she says, come to symbolize the "embodiment of paternal power and presence" and unconsciously serve the function of organizing "bodily perceptions and fantasies" into verbal constructs. These constructs help the child draw boundaries between its own and its mother's body and protect her from the regressive wish for fusion and the loss of subjective and sexual identity:

It seems evident that the transitional objects of infancy (Winnicott, 1951) give way to language as an important internal possession, capable eventually of replacing the need for the external object with thoughts about the object. . . . Over and beyond the essential importance of the role of language in structuring the human psyche, for someone who is a writer, words may come to play a specifically privileged role due to their link with unconscious bisexual fantasies. In Benedicte's case, the paralysis of her creative possibilities represented, among other aspects, an imaginary way of renouncing her secret link with her father through language and story building, a link that was forbidden by her mother. (p. 212)

Phyllis Meadow: Blocks to Experiencing Pleasure

In *The New Psychoanalysis* (2003) Meadow discusses a different but highly relevant inhibition—inhibition to experiencing pleasure, a condition that impeded progress in all the cases presented in this paper. She frames her argument in the context of both Lacanian and classical Freudian theory and argues that individuals can separate and become authentic only when they are able to take pleasure in their drives:

> The authentic, or real person, became for Lacan a pursuer of satisfaction. Prior to analysis, he is kept down by the false ideals of ego and by superego restrictions. . . . According to Lacan (1977) the fully analyzed person, freed from the desire of the Other, is able to permit himself the satisfaction of his drives. (p. 19)

Masochism, writes Meadow (2003), is a byproduct of the inability to achieve satisfaction and a prominent feature in those experiencing blocks to writing. She recounts the case of a man who "suffered . . . from a pervasive sadness," for a year after losing a brother to a drug overdose. In the course of treatment, the analyst realized that she could not encourage the "role of victim" and that this patient could not begin to pursue satisfaction in his life until he "knew what satisfaction was derived from his position as 'the one who suffers.'" "The relationship between his desire to be his mother's special boy" (p. 20) and the torment in family life created by his brother's lifelong illness continues to interfere or inhibit drive satisfaction.

Perversion is a second byproduct of frustrated drive satisfaction and also very much evident in the cases I will present. "The pervert," writes Meadow (2003), "suffers from the same anxiety over symbolic castration as the neurotic; however, his defense is disavowal." The disavowal in this case is the "pervert's unwillingness to accept the differences between the sexes" that "result in the boy allowing himself only that jouissance that falls short of genital union" (p. 21).

For Meadow (2003), then, helping a patient achieve drive satisfaction points to the road to cure. Ultimately, individuation and psychic change can happen only when "the analysand is taught that he or she will come to exist separately from the analyst (the Other) when he accepts himself as a subject of enjoyment" (p. 93).

The Love of Reading and the Writing Process

Envy can also be a crippling inhibition to writing. This is a key observation of Bonnie Friedman (1993), a writer who casts her argument in a Kleinian mold, in *Writing Past Dark: Envy, Fear, Distraction, and Other Dilemmas in the Writer's Life* (1993). In this memoir, Friedman connects the love of reading shared by writers to difficulties in writing. Reading is, of course, a necessary precursor to writing, and reading a good book—fiction or non-fiction— can be a transporting experience akin to being suckled at the breast. When in the midst of the process, I have noticed, we feel engrossed, transported, filled up; we "absorb" the text and are "nourished" by it when the experience is a particularly positive one. But as writers, we often feel discouraged when we set out to write something we hope will move our readers in the same way our favorite authors have moved us. Inspiration turns to self-defeat, procrastination, and self-flagellation. We tell ourselves we're no good at it, we have no right to attempt something so patently out of reach, we get dumb and lazy and quickly find ourselves oscillating between desire and disappointment. We put off the writing, waiting for the moment of inspiration, only to find that we have procrastinated ourselves into months of nonactivity. Friedman describes the dilemma between desire and renunciation:

> It was my very commitment to writing that kept me from it. I wanted so much for it to be that ideal, submerged experience that I put it off. I saved it up. I longed for it, missed it, got bitchy about it, petulant, then, again thought of it with a pang—an adored but long-lost love. (p. 11)

My Story

I decided to include a narrative of my own writing history in this paper, because, frankly, I couldn't write about anyone else until my own tortured journey was clear in my mind and on paper. It was the first section of the paper that I wrote, and although I debated leaving it out, I ultimately chose to include it because I believe it is similar in substance, if not detail, to the story of many of the doctoral and psychoanalytic candidates I have worked with for more than a decade. Everyone who undertakes writing a thesis, final project, or dissertation carries within them attitudes, beliefs, and experiences about writing and completion that affect every phase of the project. As we have seen in the literature review, there is something about the magnitude and significance of a written document demonstrating proficiency that induces regression, ambivalence, and a questioning of one's very being. I recommend that anyone experiencing writing difficulties take the time to commit to paper an account tracing the vicissitudes of one's writing history. It will take the focus away from the project itself but will nonetheless engage the person in the writing process and may make him or her aware of patterns not yet fully identified.

Words have always intrigued and awed me. Their mystery and power have held me in their thrall. My verbal skills have always surpassed my physical prowess. My mother liked to say that I spoke months before I walked. Sicilian was my first language, an ancient language incorporating aspects of the Greek, Latin, Arabic, and Spanish cultures of the conquerors who had all left their mark on the island. Italian—"standard," Tuscan Italian—was my second language, the language of Dante taught in school and heard on the radio. Italian was the language I learned to read and the vernacular spoken by people of education and culture. For a Sicilian, my father spoke Italian well—he had spent several years in the port city of Genoa during World War II and had become comfortable with its rhythms. At the age of eight, newly arrived in the United States, I learned English quickly—the idea of not being able to communicate was abhorrent to me—a process that in retrospect seems to have happened miraculously, without any purposefulness on my part. One moment I spoke no English; two years later I was fluent.

During that time I discovered the pleasure of reading. Books introduced me to American families who lived in Vermont, ran inns and skied for many months out of the year. They were populated by gentle mothers and fathers and clever children who were kind, generous, and fun loving, a sharp contrast to my life in a family struggling to come to terms with an America that was harsher and more alienating than anything we could have imagined when the decision to leave Sicily was made. These books were a great comfort to me. They made me feel safe and hopeful despite the unspoken, aching loss my parents, my siblings, and I felt for the home, language, and people left behind.

In high school I discovered Emily Bronte, Jane Austen, and J. D. Salinger, read them with delight, and began to study Italian as a "foreign" language. Despite my familiarity with the language, this was my first experience with the systematic study of grammar—nouns, pronouns, adjectives, verbs, and adverbs—all building blocks of verbal and written discourse. This endeavor had a psychological payoff. I had finally found a subject my mother could help me with, and it mended to a degree our often combative and fractured relationship. When I went off to college, chosen specifically because it offered a major in Italian, I began to study Italian literature, a subject with which I was unfamiliar. At the time it seemed like a good idea, a way to capitalize on an interest and advantage I had in a country in which I still often felt like an outsider. I now see this choice as an attempt to reclaim my heritage and to integrate the various aspects of my cultural history. Reading the great Italian authors, Boccaccio, Dante, Petrarca, Macchiavelli, Lampedusa, Pirandello, gave me a sense of pride and provided a counterweight to the shame I felt in my immigrant status and in the fact that my first language was a "dialect," despised by Italians and Americans both.

However, even though I seemed to make good progress, I suffered from an almost crippling fear of writing. I put off writing papers as long as possible, often producing them in a fevered state the night before they were due, panic-stricken and delirious. It was almost as though I was addicted to the near-death experience described by Joseph (1982) in "Addiction to Near-Death." I was terrified of criticism, of being unmasked as a fraud, of being stripped of my self-esteem, of being irreparably crushed. I wanted to write the papers, fuss over them lovingly, craft them to perfection—but would not and could not. They were always written in a slapdash way, never reread for content, and turned in with the hope that a miracle would happen and that I would beat the odds once again. It mostly worked. I never did as well as I could have had I taken the time to organize my thoughts or develop my argument, but I did well enough. My written English was never as good as I imagined when I thought about the papers prior to composing them, partially, I think, because I still had Sicilian and Italian syntax and cadences in my head. I was always bitterly disappointed in my written productions; I hated myself too much to be able to work constructively on improvements. The requirement that I write my literature papers in Italian in college didn't help build my skill or confidence level either. My Italian was worse than my English but I got through the program with liberal use of quotes from Italian critical texts and a kind professor. Since I was the only Italian major that year, I often had this wonderful woman to myself—a Jewish Italian aristocratic scholar who had escaped Fascist Italy—an intimate learning experience I have been able to repeat only in a personal analysis.

This fear of writing followed me to Columbia graduate school where I was admitted to the doctoral program in Italian Literature. I remember jumping with joy when I discovered at registration that the master-level thesis requirement had been dropped (Columbia too must have felt defeated by the many students who couldn't complete long writing projects) and that four class papers had been substituted in its place. Although I knew that I wanted to concentrate on the work of Luigi Pirandello, a fellow Sicilian who was awarded the 1936 Nobel Prize in literature, I still had no idea what, if anything, I had to say about him. I had fallen madly in love with his work my sophomore year in college; he was the first writer I had ever read who described the universe and conflicts of my childhood in an Italian that, although "standard," had the cadence and syntax of our native Sicilian. He also treated his subject matter in a psychodynamic way, a perspective that instinctively appealed to me years prior to my formal study of psychoanalysis. Individual perception, reality, illusion, alienation, madness, the disintegration of the self—these were all topics that he grappled with and that mesmerized me.

I whizzed through the program—classes, papers (my new husband was now my editor), Latin and French comprehension exams, written and doctoral orals—teaching undergraduate Italian language classes the whole while. But I hit a wall when it came time to concentrate seriously on writing my dissertation. My teaching contract at Columbia was up—I had surpassed the four-year limit—and my half-hearted attempts to find another teaching position proved futile. Thus, I found myself cast out, bereft, alone, and afraid.

All my unresolved conflicts around dependence and autonomy blocked me from being able to figure out how to organize a large writing project such as a dissertation. It couldn't be done overnight or even over the course of a few days, even though I often fantasized that I would hole myself up over the weekend and complete the project. My solution to this dilemma was to abandon the project and begin the study of psychoanalysis, a subject of great interest to me and a move that I hoped would free me from this painful impasse.

Once again, I quickly and successfully progressed through the analytic program and gave birth to two sons, but once again hit a wall when it came time to write the final research project, a demonstration of an in-depth understanding of my control case and, ultimately, my competence as an analyst. Finishing was difficult. Writing a lengthy case study was hell. However, after I was able to complete my final project and, several years later, my doctoral dissertation on Pirandello, I immediately began to work with candidates and graduate students experiencing many of the difficulties I describe. My understanding of what enabled me to complete these two projects and replace my suffering with the more direct pleasure of writing will be discussed at the conclusion of this paper.

In the clinical portion of the paper that follows, I will present three cases that illustrate various stages in the dissertation-writing process. In each phase the writer faces different challenges and milestones and must successfully negotiate the demands of the environment and the standards of the university. However, as I did in the psychoanalytic literature review, I focus my discussion on the investigation of internal conflicts. My analysis will be loosely organized around four indicators:

1. Dominant fantasy of meaning and significance of doctoral dissertation
2. Evidence of drive fusion or defusion
3. Sexual identity and object choice difficulties
4. Potential for drive satisfaction

Clinical Vignettes

BEGINNING PHASE: AMANDA

Amanda, a woman in her mid-forties, has been in treatment with me, on and off, for six years. She has yet to begin writing her dissertation. During the first two years of treatment she wrote a lengthy, very personal proposal, a memoir really, outlining her thoughts, ideas, and experiences about social work, a field she has been studying for well over a decade, but one she has not actually practiced. She did not discuss the contents of the proposal with me and has never shown it to me, but reported that it was well received by her advisor and that she was instructed to begin a literature review to determine what others have written on the topic, an endeavor she has yet to begin. Prior to this doctoral program she has pursued graduate studies in various disciplines and has several advanced degrees, but it appears that her academic pursuits have always been motivated by a desire to study with teachers who are important in their field. Initially her admiration for these "stars" borders on idolatry, but in time these mentors betray her and her love turns invariably into hatred. The original—adored then despised dissertation mentor—has since retired; the new advisor is considered well meaning but ineffectual.

Over time the overarching fantasy that keeps her connected to this project has revealed itself to me. It appears that the choice of dissertation topic and its fantasized outcome originate from a desire, both conscious and unconscious, to return to the idyllic days of her infancy and early childhood in a small Maine fishing village, a community populated by kindly neighbors, doting grandparents, and parents not yet overburdened by the birth of their other children. Her ambivalence about completing the project and returning to her fantasized roots is the subject of her recent sessions. She subscribes to her hometown newspaper and uses her computer time searching for a little home to call her own rather than writing her dissertation.

Amanda exhibits evidence of many examples of drive defusion. She has difficulty loving and hating the same person and splits between worshiping and feeling persecuted by objects. Political and religious paranoia often deplete her of energy for constructive pursuits. She lives in chaos. I have come to understand her inability to begin the literature review as an unwillingness to be penetrated by ideas other than her own. She claims the victim role in her family and at her job and has little awareness of her own hostility or potential for destructive action. She considers herself a kind and generous friend. In treatment, she refuses to use the couch and has "taken a break" from treatment for several months at a time if I ask a probing question.

She has been involved in a succession of inappropriate relationships with men, most of whom are married or are well-known figures in their field. She will follow these men with puppy-dog devotion until it becomes painfully clear that her devotion will never be returned in the way she would like. During the most productive (in terms of writing) period of the treatment, she spent her time discussing her wish to have a child with her married tennis coach, a man she idolizes to this day. The onset of early menopause was a traumatic event for her and put an end to these fantasies. This foreclosure of the possibility of bearing a child, I believe, also contributed to her reluctance to undertake the serious work of writing a dissertation. Several male relatives have doctorates and are distinguished in their field, and although she is happy to bask in their reflected glory, she is convinced she will never be able to match their achievements. Lately she has begun to wonder if she is a lesbian, after a friend suggested that her persecutory anxiety about a mutual friend meant she had sexual feelings for her.

This patient achieves drive satisfaction perversely from activities other than dissertation writing. She writes often and well on topics totally unrelated to her project and spends days crafting and polishing essays on subjects that come to consume her. She routinely brings these productions into the sessions for me to admire. She also obtains perverse pleasure from a relationship with a man who is more than willing to engage in foreplay with her but refuses to have genital sex with her. Whenever she fantasizes about leaving New York to return to her fishing village, it is her love for this man, she says, that keeps her here. My work with her centers on the question, "Should I help you to dedicate yourself to the dissertation or to abandon it?" The answer to this question is yet unclear.

MIDDLE PHASE: ELIZABETH

Elizabeth is also in her mid-forties and has been in treatment for about five years. She too has been pursuing doctoral studies for well over a decade and began with me at a time of great personal crisis: Her marriage was at a crossroads because of her refusal to have a child, a position she had held firmly from the onset of the marriage and one to which her husband had agreed but was now asking her to reconsider. After her husband renounced his desire for a child, she called me, seeking help with her dissertation, telling me that although a domestic crisis had been averted, she was in a state of panic about her studies. She had spent several years writing a proposal on a topic ultimately deemed untenable by an advisor who instructed her to read the recent literature if she wanted to make the study relevant. This assessment was a terrible blow, and she subsequently abandoned both the topic and the advisor. She was also prompted to seek my help because she had just received a letter threatening to drop her from the program if she did not make significant progress on her dissertation.

She did not want to give up. In the treatment room she appeared brittle, constricted, and depressed. The capriciousness of her advisor and her own stupidity were to blame for her troubles. How could she begin to research a new topic she would not know was acceptable until she committed her ideas to paper? The uncertainly of the process, her harsh superego, and her fear of rejection had such a stranglehold on her that she was unable to write a single word for many months.

The fantasy that keeps her both connected and unable to finish this project, I believe, has to do with her conflict between a wish and a fear of being accepted, despite her hatred of children and ultimately of herself. During our last session she told me that she was reluctant to attend her high school reunion because she was afraid that if she told her classmates that she had not yet finished her dissertation, their opinion of her would be confirmed—she was "weird" and did have "two heads" after all. What made her weird, she said, was her interest in esoteric subjects and the fact that she told others that she never intended to have children. And yet, I have come to realize, not completing the dissertation serves to keep her in a childlike state, one she bemoans but takes no consistent steps to leave behind. She muses that completing her dissertation will finally give her entry into the world of adults but wonders what it will be like to be a grown-up.

In Elizabeth's case there is evidence of both drive fusion and defusion. She both loves and hates her husband and is growing increasingly comfortable with her anger. During the past five years she has been successful in formulating a viable research study and has been awarded several fellowships to study abroad to collect data for her anthropological study. She has several accepted dissertation chapters and with consistent effort could bring the project to completion. She works in her field and actively seeks positions in geographical areas that appeal to her. However, she still engages in masochistic behavior and often falls into a state of hopelessness about the prospects for her future.

She swore she would never be a nag like her mother. Growing up, she thought her siblings were brats and found solace in a world of fantasy. However, she could never aspire to be like her accomplished father, a physicist of superior intellect who completed his studies ahead of everyone else. She married a man who, although supportive of her interests, is a passive underachiever, a source of great disappointment to her, and the subject of many of her sessions. In a recent group session after attending a reception where wine was served, she revealed that both she and her husband are bisexual and have in the past engaged in relations with the same person. She consciously chose heterosexuality because her male partner proved to be much kinder than her female partner.

This patient gains drive satisfaction in writing the dissertation when she allows herself to engage in the process, but when procrastinating she takes perverse pleasure in playing video games and rereading favorite novels. Her superego prohibits her from the pleasure of reading something new. She, too, spends a great deal of time and effort writing lengthy essays on topics marginally related to her topic. Her fear of rejection interferes with her ability to get help from her advisor and from me. She rarely talks about the dissertation to me or anyone else, and when pressed, she will complain that no one is interested in her work. She has cut back on her individual sessions because of financial constraints but continues to work with me in a therapy group setting— her schedule, she says, does not permit her to attend the dissertation group.

COMPLETION PHASE: LOUISE

Louise was referred to me by her analyst a year ago to help her overcome blocks to completing her dissertation. She is in her mid-thirties and has been enrolled in a graduate program for nearly ten years. Her many years of individual and group therapy have made her self-aware and articulate. However, when feeling neglected or criticized, she invariably responds with a powerful wish to die, and although nearly finished with her project, she is prepared to abandon it at a moment's notice when things go badly.

With no prompting, she was able to tell me the fantasy that propelled her to pursue doctoral studies. She consciously enrolled in graduate school in order to make herself more desirable to men who she hoped would appreciate her talents, intelligence, and accomplishments. Underlying this fantasy is, of course, a bedrock fear of not being desirable, talented, intelligent, or accomplished. Whenever she feels frustrated with the length and difficulty of the dissertation-writing process, she returns to this fantasy and berates herself mercilessly.

She exhibits a high degree of drive fusion in some areas, but when under stress, the strength of her death drive is a powerful, annihilating force. She is competent in many areas, well organized, and uses the sessions to help her accomplish her well-formulated goals. However, she comes completely undone when she feels unappreciated, neglected, or criticized. She rails against those who injure her, but her sadism, I have noticed, is most often turned against the self. She is also overcome with envy of people who have the things she wants: a partner, a child, and a successful career. She reports that she was an adored and accomplished child, but when her parents suddenly abandoned their parental duties and became self-involved, she began to behave in self-destructive ways. She is now vigilant about diet and exercise, necessary ingredients to a successful day of writing.

Louise has had a series of relationships that for one reason or another have not lasted. She has also had a series of advisors who have gotten ill or abused her trust, and this too has slowed her down and continues to be a great source of resentment. She worries that her age will prohibit her from finding a suitable partner in time to have children. Her father, who is ABD to this day, is not a presence in her life, and her mother, a respected but narcissistic performer, is the object of both admiration and scorn.

This patient is capable of great drive satisfaction and takes great pleasure in her writing. She is often happiest when working on her dissertation and feels frustrated when other matters impinge on her time. This intolerance for distractions from the project is common to all the dissertators I have worked with in the final writing phase—a phase in which the thesis becomes all-consuming. However, until recently, Louise chose isolation, miserable and alone, convinced that non-graduate students could not possibly understand her plight. This is quite common in some dissertators, and I have come to understand this self-imposed exile as an attempt to ward off powerful feelings of shame around unacceptable longings to have others know and care about your work. Happily, since joining my dissertation group, Louise has become more social and has even started dating again, realizing anew the great pleasure she takes in being with a man and sharing her many interests with him.

My Story Revisited

My journey follows the same course described in the three cases above. I initially struggled to find an appropriate topic for my dissertation, but more importantly, I struggled to come to terms with my dominant fantasy—that completing a PhD would bestow me with a penis, something I both feared and desired. I also had the fantasy that a doctorate would bring me great prestige and protect me from criticism, both from within and without.

Realizing in my analysis that my gender would not be altered and that completing the project would not immunize me from daily struggles, I was then able to demystify the process and come to view the dissertation as simply another academic task that needed to be completed. Once I realized that I wanted to pursue it for its own sake and for career advancement, I allowed myself to know that I wanted it more than life itself.

I became driven to complete it. In my experience, no one finishes a difficult and lengthy project such as a dissertation without a monumental assertion of will. I kept my destructive impulses at bay by keeping them front and center in my mind. An event comes to mind that vividly illustrates the hold that the death drive had on me when I was totally blocked from even imagining what I could possibly say about Pirandello that would contribute to the existing literature. Sitting in the institute library one day, I found myself crying inconsolably because I had just realized that the reason I couldn't write about Pirandello was because I wanted to destroy him and his distinguished reputation. At that moment he became a stand-in for my father whom I loved and admired but who confided too much in me and put too many demands on me; it was he who wanted me to be a doctor, after all, a goal I might never have pursued on my own. This realization freed me and sparked my interest in sublimation, a mechanism essential to anyone pursuing academic work.

My sexual identity became solidified after I bore two children, an accomplishment that far overshadows anything else I have ever done. Having healthy children gave me the confidence that I could create something of value. An unexpected byproduct of motherhood was the realization that now that I had no time to waste; my uncertainty about what to do with my life suddenly disappeared. I become resolute in my desire to be an analyst and in my desire to one day complete my doctoral studies.

I derived great satisfaction from researching and writing the dissertation. The more I surrendered to the process, the more pleasure I derived from it. The project became an act of integration synthesizing my interests in preoedipal conflicts with my interests in the life and work of Pirandello. I found that I loved the solitude of research and the thrill of discovery. The writing process was difficult initially, but the more I did it, the better I got at it and the more I enjoyed it. My students and patients report the same thing. Writing is a skill that can be honed and polished and one that gets easier with practice. I believe that ABDs suffer more when not writing than when writing; doing is more satisfying than not doing. Students enrolled in doctoral programs deserve to give themselves the maturational experience of finishing what they started.

Concluding Remarks

As has been discussed, writing blocks emanate from various sources, but they are all conceptualized within a dynamic framework—as a struggle between two equally powerful forces battling for supremacy. For Freud, inhibitions to creativity were initially formulated as originating from the conflicting demands of the pleasure and reality principles and later of the life and death drives; Rank viewed writing blocks as expressions of ambivalence resulting from the birth trauma, a struggle between individuation and a desire for fusion; Hannah Segal, Melanie Klein's disciple, argued that artistic inhibitions were the result of the inability to overcome depressive anxiety, a condition emanating from a conflict between innate destructiveness and the fear of object loss; and Joyce McDougall introduced the element of sexual identity and theorized that writing inhibitions resulted from the trauma of early object loss and its accompanying disturbances in the capacity for ambisexual identifications. These theories build on and complement each other, and elements of each have served to illuminate aspects of the cases presented in this paper.

My clinical discussion focused on four indicators: dominant fantasy, evidence of drive fusion, sexual identity disturbances, and the potential for drive satisfaction—concepts extracted from the literature review and a framework within which to organize the case material. From this small sample I propose these preliminary findings:

1. The more conscious the fantasy of the symbolic meaning of the dissertation, the greater likelihood that writing impasses can be overcome
2. The more capacity one has for drive fusion and sublimation, the better the prognosis for completion
3. The fewer difficulties one exhibits in sexual identity and object choices, the easier the process of creation will be
4. The greater the potential for drive satisfaction, the more one will enjoy the writing process and the greater the likelihood that the dissertation will be completed in a timely fashion

In this paper I have limited myself to an investigation of the origins and meaning of blockage and have presented case material that illustrates these theoretical constructs. However, I did not address the issue of how one treats inhibitions to writing, the questions one asks and the interventions that work—in short, the technique of curing writing blocks. It would also be useful to study the meaning of enactments as they occur in the treatment and the patient's capacity for connectedness, another possible indicator of the ability to keep the project alive in the mind and bring it to a successful conclusion.

REFERENCES

Crews, F. (1975), *Out of My System: Psychoanalysis, Ideology and Critical Method*. New York: Oxford University Press.

Dyer, G. (1997), *Out of Sheer Rage: Wrestling with D. H. Lawrence*. New York: North Point Press.

Ferraro, F. (2003), Psychic bisexuality and creativity. *International Journal of Psychoanalysis*, 84:1451–1467.

Freud, S. (1910), Creative writers and daydreaming. *Standard Edition*. London: Hogarth Press, 9:141–154.

——— (1910), Leonardo da Vinci and a memory of his childhood. *Standard Edition*. London: Hogarth Press, 11:59–137.

——— (1913), The theme of the three caskets. *Standard Edition*. London: Hogarth Press, 12:289–301.

——— (1916–17), The paths to the formation of symptoms. *Standard Edition*. London: Hogarth Press, 16:58–377.

——— (1920a), The psychogenesis of a case of homosexuality in a woman. *Standard Edition*. London: Hogarth Press, 18:145–172.

——— (1920b), Beyond the pleasure principle. *Standard Edition*. London: Hogarth Press, 18:3–64.

——— (1923), The two classes of instincts. *Standard Edition*. London: Hogarth Press, 19:40–47.

——— (1926), Inhibitions, symptoms and anxiety. *Standard Edition*. London: Hogarth Press, 20:77–174.

——— (1928), Dostoevsky and parricide. *Standard Edition*. London: Hogarth Press, 21:175–196.

Friedman, B. (1993), *Writing Past Dark: Envy, Fear, Distraction, and Other Dilemmas in the Writer's Life*. New York: Harper Perennial.

Joseph, B. (1982), Addiction to near-death. *International Journal of Psychoanalysts*, 63:449–456.

Klein, M. (1975), *The Writings of Melanie Klein*. Four Volumes. London: Hogarth Press.

Lacan, J. (1977), *Ecrits: A Selection*. A. Sheridan, translator. New York: Norton.

Laplanche, J. & J. B. Pontalis (1973), *The Language of Psychoanalysis*. D. Nicholson-Smith, translator. New York: Norton.

Leader, Z. (1991), *Writer's Block*. Baltimore: John Hopkins University Press.

McDougall, J. (1989), The dead father: on early psychic trauma and its relation to disturbance in sexual identity and creative activity. *International Journal of Psychoanalysis*, 70:205-219.

———— (1991), Sexual identity, trauma and creativity. *Psychoanalytic Inquiry*, 11:559–581.

Meadow, P. W. (2003), *The New Psychoanalysis*. New York: Rowman & Littlefield.

Rank, O. (1929), *The Trauma of Birth*. New York: Harcourt Brace.

———— (1932), *Art and Artist*. Reprint. New York: Alfred A. Knopf, 1968.

Segal, H. (1952), A psychoanalytic approach to aesthetics. *International Journal of Psychoanalysis*, 33:196–207.

Winnicott, D. (1951), Transitional objects and transitional phenomena. *Collected Papers*. New York: Basic Books.

915 West End Ave. #1B
New York, NY 10025
rfmcaloon@aol.com

Modern Psychoanalysis
Vol. XXIX, No. 2, 2004

When Drives Are Dangerous: Drive Theory and Resource Overconsumption

FRANCES BIGDA-PEYTON

Overconsumption of resources has been identified as a major cause of current environmental problems. Psychoanalysts have begun shedding light on the intrapsychic and group dynamics underlying this phenomenon. Their contributions are herein reviewed. Drive theory adds an understanding of the death instinct. Humans have inherent tendencies to destroy and use up. Harmful overconsumption occurs when psychic structures dominated by destructive instincts succeed in overpowering life-sustaining impulses. Overconsumption also functions as a defense against the awareness of death wishes. Narcissistic fixations keep individuals and groups from maturing to the point of recognizing that they must give to the environment in order to be provided for in a sustainable way.

The story of King Midas whose greed for riches led him to turn his daughter into gold is well known. It is an allegory about insatiability and losing sight of human connection. Midas became aware that his material quest was wrongly aimed only after he had destroyed his child.

This story has been considered an allegory for our time (Wachtel, 2003). Americans are using up natural resources at alarming and non-sustainable rates. For example, predictions of how long oil supplies will last are dire, including those provided by the usually optimistic Department of Energy. There have been no major oil discoveries in the

© 2004 CMPS/*Modern Psychoanalysis*, Vol. 29, No. 2

U.S. in decades and oil production has been declining since the 1970s. Concurrently, U.S. oil demand is huge and increasing. With less than five percent of the world's population, Americans consume more than 25 percent of the world's oil supplies. Overconsumption is evident in other sectors as well. Average house size has grown though family size has decreased. A growing number of Americans are obese, making weight-related illnesses a major cause of preventable deaths. Increasingly, many Americans organize their lives around escalating standards of consumption. It is doubtful that this is beneficial to individuals, their relationships, or the environment.

Polls confirm these reservations about our consumer culture. A 1995 report (Farrell, 2003) showed that "we believe that materialism, greed, and selfishness increasingly dominate American life, crowding out a more meaningful set of values centered on family, responsibility, and community." Eighty-six percent of respondents thought that "today's youth are too focused on consuming and buying things." Eighty-two percent agreed that "most of us buy and consume far more than we need" (p. 268).

Literature Review

Psychoanalytic concepts have been routinely used to explain aspects of overconsumption (Winter, 1996). There is evidence, for instance, that denial and projection underlie overconsumption. Schor (1998) found that though most of her survey respondents regarded the general population as materialistic, they rated themselves as "less materialistic." Respondents resisted recognizing the extent to which they followed the lead of others. Being motivated to consume to achieve social status was routinely attributed to others. Respondents also denied that they tried to "keep up with the Jones" despite statistical evidence to the contrary.

Increasingly, psychoanalytic writers have entered this discussion of pathological consumption. Wachtel (2003), a leader in this debate, has examined the ways social forces and intrapsychic dynamics reciprocally shape one another through the mechanism of introjection. When parents approve of or reward a child's behavior, that behavior, he explains, becomes introjected into an ego-ideal. Children feel pride when they act in accord with parental ideals. Wachtel posited that problems arise because the introjection of insatiable expectations is common in our culture. Nothing is enough, and more is better. Once internalized, individuals experience chronic feelings of discontent and dissatisfaction. Wachtel regarded insatiability as characteristic of societies, such as ours, that are "marked by vast opportunity, but also intense competition, enormous variations in how much wealth and income is achieved, and powerful consequences resulting from which end of the economic spectrum one ends up on" (p. 112). In a culture of increasingly divergent incomes, losing out or falling behind are high-stakes concerns (Schor, 1998).

Self-object formation also plays a significant role. Kohut viewed self-objects as the building blocks for the construction of the autonomous self. They provide experiences of validation that are necessary for the development of a stable sense of self. Wachtel (1989, 2003) has argued that many aspects of modern society, such as the absence of community, rituals, and shared values, make it difficult to find consistent sources of self-validation. He reminds us that though self-objects generally take the form of another person, they can also be objects and ideas. Money and corporations may serve as substitute self-objects. When close friendships at work change due to relocations and job restructuring, when no extended communities are available, then entities such as corporations, with their accompanying values and practices, become a constant through which to find validation. Unfortunately, seeking to sustain selfhood on this basis leaves people less able to develop alternative, more satisfying object relations. Choosing to make money or have more possessions as a measure of validation keeps a vicious cycle going. Individuals grow further alienated from human sources of nourishment. Using money to meet material needs is conscious; using it to find self-objects is largely unconscious (Kanner & Gomes, 1995).

Utilizing a related concept, Kanner and Gomes (1995) link overconsumption to the development of a false self that is consumer oriented. They label this the "all consuming self." The false self, they feel, arises from a distortion of authentic needs and desires. It is formed when a child attends to external demands and rewards in order to obtain parental approval and love. When external pressures conflict with children's own feelings, personal feelings are ignored and children come to believe that parental wishes are their own. In a similar manner, children internalize media and societal messages. They substitute what they are told to want for what they truly want. By the time they reach adulthood, authentic feelings lie buried and individuals have only the vaguest sense that something is missing. The false self masks unacknowledged longings and feelings. Gruen (1995) writes that this alienation from personal experience may account for why there would be little empathy for the environment. How can there be true empathy for externals if there is no empathy for the self? Further, he suggests that individuals may create pain in the external world in order to know their own feelings of pain.

Roszak (1992) sees a connection between socialization and exploitative environmental practices. He posits that male children are particularly vulnerable to developing exploitative tendencies because they are taught to be independent and dominant in order to be admired. Passivity is equated with humiliation and inadequacy. Psychoanalyst Nancy Chodorow (1978) has examined the implications of the emphasis on separateness in the mothering of boys. She observes males over the course of development pull away from the maternal dyad and identify with the father. Thus, their identity becomes based on the ability to disconnect and deny the importance of relationship. The Western cultural ideal of radical autonomy reinforces this push toward separateness. However, since complete autonomy is impossible, people have to interact with the demands of others. Men may develop the compromise solution of denying dependence and seeking dominance through possessions and power (Kaschak, 1992).

Some object relations critiques of child-rearing practices have environmental implications. For example, when infants are made to spend time alone, separated from primary caregivers, and are given bottles rather than breast-fed and then given a world of playthings, they learn to seek security in material things instead of the reassurance that comes from cherished people (Schmookler, 2003). Having found mixed comfort from the mother, they seek comfort in material possessions.[1] Overconsumption, then, is both a repetition of damaged early attachments and a defense against longings. Particular forms reflect dealings with early objects and fantasies associated with them. Individuals' relationship with our planet (*mother* earth) mirrors their original relationship with caregivers (Winter, 2000).

Psychoanalysts have suggested that trauma, and the defensive splitting that can accompany it, helps explain our environmental predicament. For instance, Velikovsky (1982), Shepherd (1995), and Metzner (1993) suggest many large-scale traumas that might have created disconnection from the natural world: the domestication of nature (the economic movement from hunting and gathering to farming); the Black

---

[1]Anthropologists and economists have elaborated upon this hypothesis. For example, they place child-rearing practices in an overall cultural context arising from the seventeenth-century ideology depicting society as a marketplace primarily designed for exchange among individuals. This ideology has worked to erode non-contractual bonds among people (Schmookler, 2003).

Death wiping out one-third of the population of the fourteenth century; and cataclysmic natural events leading to massive loss of life and forced migration. Such events may have produced a permanent fear and insecurity among humans regarding their relationship to the Earth. Velikovsky argued that memories of harmony and connection with nature thus became repressed and split off.

Analysts who focus on the impact of trauma infer that destructive behavior is the result of poorly integrated or repressed memories and affect. Those traumatized need to mourn, deal with their guilt about survival, or succumb to despair or denial (Nicholson, 2002). Lifton (1967) identified apathy and psychic numbing as chief defenses against overwhelming feelings associated with cataclysmic events. People become mute in the face of catastrophe. Nicholson poetically argued that a large part of our relationship with nature transpires in silence. Nature is a place where people find an intangible presence—as with the mother, a place to experience separation and merger, the expansive nature of the other, and the loss of the self. This preverbal relationship may further contribute to the inability to speak about personal actions that might harm the environment. Nicholson's work is derived from the ideas of Winnecott (1963) and Searles (1960) that the material world is entwined with our original experience of home and self. Nature provides an early, containing mental space. Separation away from the natural world occurs gradually as the child develops in time and space. The role of the physical world in human development often remains unacknowledged and unarticulated.

Defensive splitting is problematic insofar as nature comes to be seen as "the other"—an entity onto which desires can be projected without injury to the self. Tarnas (1989) and Keepin (2003) have reviewed the intellectual history of "cosmological alienation" throughout Western philosophy (that is, mankind's perception of being distinct from nature, a primary self-object split). If people see nature as apart from themselves and view their purpose as conquering it to promote civilization (Freud, 1930), then exploitation is justified. Lakoff (2002) identifies this as the "conservative" moral viewpoint. Nature is there for human exploitation; rewards go to those who are disciplined, industrious, and dominant. Unfortunately, this perspective misses fundamental ecological and systems research regarding human interconnection with the natural world.

Another relevant contribution is the notion of a repressed "ecological unconscious" (Roszak, 1992) or what Lifton (1976) calls "the species self." This refers to an unconscious repository of wisdom about interdependence with nature. In his original idea of the collective unconscious (Aizenstat, 1995), Jung proposed the notion of a broader unconscious, consisting of prehuman animal and biological archetypes. Later, Jung emphasized pan-human religious symbols and Jungian practice became centered almost exclusively on the human psyche— personal and collective. Jung referred to the connection of the psyche with the outer world in other parts of his work. For example, in his idea of "psychoid" phenomena, Jung hypothesized that an archetype can exist in both psychic and physical states.

The biologist Edward O. Wilson (1984) concurs with the notion of an ecological unconscious. He claims that what has been repressed in modern humans is an innate "biophiliac instinct . . . an innate tendency to focus on life and lifelike processes" (p. 1). Wilson sees the drive to be connected to and understands the natural world as being on a par with aggressive and sexual drives. Just as psychoanalysis led the way in addressing the repression of sexuality, eco-psychological writers urge that attention be paid to the species unconscious that lies within humans (Winter, 2000). This perspective also considers the possibility of the psychic reality and consciousness of nonhuman phenomena and the possible effects these have on human consciousness. This area is beginning to receive research attention (Felch, 2003).

Finally, the contributions of group analysts are relevant, though a review of these is beyond the scope of this paper. Nicholson (2002) summarizes these in *The Love of Nature and the End of the World.* Briefly, she writes that humans, being socially oriented, have been shown to take immediate and, at times ill-founded, actions because of tendencies toward "group think." In other words, they go along with group standards unquestioningly. Groups also demonstrate tendencies toward (and accompanying fantasies about) reliance on the "wise" group leader for guidance. An interesting socio-analytic hypothesis is that cultures are founded on violent sacrifice. Nicholson points out that American fantasies center on overcoming and exploiting nature. At an unconscious level, then, American group cohesion may result from the continued sacrifice of nature, that is, exploitation is necessary for social survival unless another fantasy is embraced.

What Do Drives Have to Do with It?

The relevance of drive theory to understanding overconsumption has been downplayed in the literature. Wachtel (2003) goes so far as to say that aspects of drive theory are useless. For instance, regarding Klein's notions of greed being related to infantile fantasies of devouring and destroying the breast, a drive- and object-based perspective, he writes, "[this formulation] provides little that is of any use for exploring links between psychological experience and broader social issues. [Kleinian notions] . . . are far too hermetic, far too focused on an inner world that is further from the world of everyday social reality than Neptune or Pluto" (pp. 105–106).

It is the contention of this paper that drive theory offers a significant lens though which to understand why we are using natural resources at unsustainable rates. Using the drive perspective in conjunction with developmental theory illuminates a variety of motivations for overconsumption. Drive theory sheds light on the general tendencies as well as specific forms that instincts take over the course of normal and pathological development.

Freud (1915–1917) believed that inborn life and death instincts played a much larger role in personality development than contextual factors. They drive behavior. In general, external stimuli pose fewer demands and require less complicated forms of accommodation than drives. It is easier to flee from the external demands of a situation than a biological need. Freud's model is tension-reducing. Behavior is activated by internal irritation and subsides when appropriate action diminishes this stimulation. The aim of the instinct is to return the individual to a prior state of relative quiescence. Due to the nature of drives, the individual is compelled to repeat cycles of excitation and quiescence.

Freud (1923) also argued that behavior resulted from the interaction between the structures of the id, ego, and superego. Each has its own properties and mechanisms that can be difficult to disentangle since each impacts behavior. The id, the reservoir of psychic energy, is the original biological system that contains the instincts. Relevant to the present discussion, it operates on the pleasure principle whose aim is to obtain pleasure and avoid pain. The id produces the desire to consume in order to meet life-sustaining needs as well as the desire to fulfill other life-promoting impulses (e.g., love, sex, self-preservation, constancy of energy levels, and the creation and maintenance of more differentiated, organized relationships). The id is also the repository of the death instincts that seek to destroy and kill. These instincts push for disunity, equalization of tension, and a return to a void, inorganic state. It is only through the workings of the life instinct that destructive impulses are directed outward. The drives mix to varying extents and are rarely seen in pure forms. The workings of the death instincts can be less conspicuous than libidinal urges.

Freud's (1920) most famous formulation of the death instinct was: "The goal of all life is death" (p. 38). In "Beyond the Pleasure Principle," he posited an inwardly-directed death instinct, a wish to return to the stability of the inorganic world that was based on Fechner's (1848) constancy principle. He argued that living matter evolved by the action of cosmic forces upon inorganic matter. These changes were relatively unstable at first and quickly reverted to their prior inorganic state. Gradually, as evolutionary changes occurred, the length of life increased though it always finally regressed to the stability of inorganic systems. Living beings could reproduce; they did not have to depend upon being created out of inorganic matter. Yet even so, he argued, living beings inevitably obey the constancy principle that governs their existence. This tendency is expressed in an organism as an instinctive drive toward death. As sobering as this seems, the theory suggests a conflict with life-giving activity. Humans embody conflicting impulses, to preserve vital unities and to undo life.

Aggression is the most visible derivative of the death instinct. It presses for discharge in the same way as libidinal urges though its tendency is in the opposite direction. Frustration serves as its vehicle. (In other words, aggression is not simply a reaction to frustrated pleasure-seeking.) Aggression arises spontaneously or when defensive controls to hold it in check are overrun (the structural perspective). It also arises when fusion with libidinal drives is insufficient to balance it and appropriate outlets for its expression have not been achieved (the modern drive perspective). An example of unfused death instinct is observed in the wish to die. Freud's (1930) strongest depiction of the aggressive instinct appears in "Civilization and Its Discontents":

> men are not gentle creatures who want to be loved, and who at the most can defend themselves if they are attacked: they are, on the contrary, creatures among whose instinctual endowments is to be reckoned a powerful share of aggressiveness. As a result, their neighbor is for them not only a potential helper or sexual object, but also someone who tempts them to satisfy their aggressiveness on him, to exploit his capacity for work without compensation, to use him sexually without his consent, to seize his possessions, to humiliate him, to cause him pain, to torture and kill him. . . . In circumstances that are favourable to it, when the mental counter-forces which ordinarily inhibit it are out of action, it also manifests itself spontaneously and reveals man as a savage beast to whom consideration towards his own kind is something alien. (pp. 111–112)

In terms of the present discussion, destroying resources and perceiving others as competitors to be outdone are the product of aggressive impulses. Whether the impulses are expressed in their purest manifestations will depend on drive endowment and the combinations of drive fusion/defusion that have been established at various points in development.

Structural Theory

Structural theory makes a useful contribution to understanding the dynamics underlying overconsumption. "The life drive leads individuals to do anything to stay alive. They will assimilate, accommodate, or make structural internal changes to preserve life" (Meadow, 2003, p. 28). Libidinal tendencies to consume and aggressive tendencies to destroy would run rampant if the ego-ideal (a part of the superego) encouraged consumption without limits. This might occur if the cultural ideal suggested that people could have it all and were entitled to it. This is exactly the description of current consumer attitudes depicted in business texts (e.g., Silverstein & Fiske, 2003). Further problems arise if the id is continuously overaroused as might be expected in the face of pervasive advertising. In fact, Schor (1998) reports that increased television watching is directly related to increased spending.

The ego prevents the discharge of tension until an appropriate object is discovered. Its challenge is to mediate the demands of the id with those of the superego. In approaching the issue of overconsumption, the crucial question is whether the ego can, in the process of seeking gratification, consider what the external world also needs in order to give the individual pleasure. Trouble results if this knowledge is blocked out. A well-researched example is the "tragedy of the commons" dilemma in which individuals, confronted with the hypothetical problem of allocating a fixed resource, show tendencies to look out only for personal interests and neglect the fact that others might be doing the same (Hardin, 1968). This strategy results in rapidly depleted resources. Individuals must consider the needs of others, the external environment, and themselves if they are to obtain sustainable gratification. It is possible that the ego might not be adequately trained to understand the long-term consequences of consumer actions. As a result, individuals fail to achieve the balance necessary to support the needs of the self and the requirements of the environment.

Fenichel (1945) views behavior as the result of (1) the external stimuli to which we react, (2) our physical state which produces internal stimuli and determines the intensity and mode of our reactions, (3) our conceptual goals, in other words, our thoughts about what we want to do and say, and (4) the derivatives of warded-off impulses that are seeking discharge. Adding further complexity to this model is the appreciation that no part of the personality is conflict-free. Conflicts can be observed between physical states, impulses, conceptual goals and ideals, and perceived ways of achieving results.

Drive Theory

Meadow (2003) regards drive theory as more parsimonious than the structural approach. Drive theory emphasizes the importance of the quantitative aspect of instincts, temperament, and energy flow. It posits that personality evolves from the energy flow between the two sets of drives, each searching for dominance. At various points in development, individuals mature in the functions that enable drive satisfaction and fusion. This is observed in activities and enactments. Pathology occurs when aggressive drives are not adequately fused with life-seeking impulses. A clinical example is individuals who cannot find immediate outlets for aggressive discharge, especially outlets that are life enhancing. In the most virulent form, individuals become severely narcissistic and violent, seeking to die or withdrawing into flooded mental conditions of nothingness (Spotnitz, 1976; Rosenfeld, 1971).

Death instincts directed at the environment without regard for sustaining life suggest a self that is almost completely overpowered by aggressive tendencies. Inadequately fused, aggressive drives are projected outward and take such forms as self-destructive overconsumption.

The Denial of Death and Death Instincts

Ernst Becker (1997) and Norman O. Brown (1985) propose that culture functions to assuage the terror engendered by the awareness of death. It reduces death anxiety by giving individuals a sense of meaning and value in the world. It tells people how to "make something" of their lives; it provides ideas about what happens after life and symbolic means to achieve immortality (creating works of art, performing heroic, selfless deeds, etc.). Solomon, Greenberg, and Pyszczynsk (2003) think that individuals lash out at anyone who threatens existing cultural world views. Awareness of the death-denying illusions of others casts doubt on the truth of personal views about such matters. Rather that accept the inevitability of death directly (and no longer tying up psychic energy repressing feelings about it), people seek to destroy those who threaten their world perspectives. This enables personal, death-denying illusions to be maintained.

Do people strike out against the natural world because the inevitability of death is so evident in nature? Repression of death awareness is challenging to maintain in the face of the demise of family members, seasonal changes, cataclysmic natural occurrences, and aging. Symbolically, to accept nature's limits represents accepting personal limits. If individuals treat natural resources as limitless, then they can maintain the illusion of their own limitlessness. Destroying nature is preferable to becoming aware of death and the wish for it.

Pollack's (1999) important work on how the unconscious shapes research suggests another way that denying death and death instincts could be detrimental to the environment. Researchers and policy makers who block out this knowledge might focus instead on developing new ways to extract declining resources instead of examining how to find satisfaction in a world of limited resources. Unconscious factors determine what is studied and what is not. In failing to recognize internal forces (in particular, the wish to destroy and concurrent fantasies of omnipotence and escaping death and suffering), fuller and more satisfying solutions are not considered.

Adding the Developmental Perspective

Melanie Klein's (1955) stages of development have implications for what motivates overconsumption for those fixated at different maturational levels. For example, unconscious attitudes and anxieties could be projected onto the environment as a result of inadequately having worked through the depressive stage. Searles (1972) hypothesized that apathy in the face of destruction speaks to there being something unfulfilling about life, essentially, not having a life worth living. Searles further argued that denying that the destruction of the earth is taking place could be used to obscure a past that the patient may not wish to remember. Modern analysts would suggest that the self-hatred characteristic of the depressive stance could be projected onto the environment as an extension of the self. Overconsumption also provides feelings of omnipotence. The illusion of creating an unspoiled world through possessions is achieved, thus relieving feelings of depression and hopelessness. During (1992) has called this the fantasy of returning to the garden.

Unconscious oedipal attitudes seem evident in not considering the survival of future generations (Searles, 1972). Unconscious envy, hatred, and fear could be motivating the destruction of formidable rivals—one's children. It may be recalled that in the Oedipus myth, not only did Oedipus seek to kill his father, but his father began the tragic unfolding by seeking the death of his son. Relinquishing evidence of genital primacy (e.g., enormous mansions and gas-guzzling vehicles) symbolizes being asked to return to the less powerful state of childhood, when genital primacy was longed for rather than achieved. Searles goes on to suggest that envy of a favored rival could also be given vicarious satisfaction by leveling the environmental playing field. Even poor people can have satisfaction in seeing that environmental destruction menaces poor and rich alike.

Preverbal conflicts, the emphasis of the modern school, are particularly relevant insofar as omnipotent, narcissistic states can become overrun by destructive instincts. In Klein's schizoid position, for instance, individuals are shielded from the recognition of the inevitability of death. Searles (1960, 1972) observed that these regressed patients displayed an unconscious wish to destroy life rather than surrender to the inevitability of losing it. Spotnitz (1976) noted that schizophrenics deny murderous impulses. The mind and outer environment are destroyed interchangeably since the schizophrenic is undifferentiated from the external world. Destroying the mind ensures that there will be nothing to lose (no death).

Rosenfeld (1971) described narcissistic patients in terms of pathological drive fusion. In order to maintain feelings of omnipotence, these patients destroy the loving part of the self (libidinal impulses) in favor of the autonomous, unrelated, and destructive drives. Paranoid individuals, for example, cannot easily integrate human and nonhuman components. Their internal struggle is projected onto the environment. They experience the predicament of being terrorized by a pervasive enemy. There is no separate self with which to struggle against this "outer" threat. In the realm of omnipotent fantasy, earth could represent reality and hinder the possibility of omnipotence (Searles, 1972).

Searles (1972) observed that preoedipal patients also demonstrate "a fear of their fantasized omnipotence lest it disqualify them from human love" (p. 371). He raised an interesting question, one that could readily be applied to this discussion: Does destructiveness directed against the environment grow out of unconscious ambivalence about our omnipotent potential? "Is it a coincidence that mankind is on the brink of environmental destruction just as it is on the threshold of breaking chains of disease and interplanetary travel? I surmise that we are powerfully drawn to suicidally polluting our planet so as to ensure our dying upon it as men, rather than existing elsewhere as—so we tend distortedly to assume—gods or robots" (pp. 371–372).

Whether or not large segments of our population is narcissistic (see Wachtel, 1989; Kanner & Gomes, 1995; and Lasch, 1979 for a fuller discussion of this issue), it does seem evident that narcissistic individuals and groups can find ways to express unfused aggressive tendencies through overconsumption.

Case Study

A clinical example of a narcissistic woman, an avid over-consumer, is illustrative. This woman longs to be comforted in recompense for all the unfairness she has suffered. Because of her tortured past, she is frustrated with the analyst for not providing free treatment. She begs for more: for the analyst to act outside of the session, for others to meet her needs selflessly, or for the analyst to convince others to do this for her. She is frustrated when friends do not provide her with supplies. She rages if they have demands of their own. She is distressed that she has to pay for vacations, that special accommodations are not made for her.

This woman lives in a world where she is psychically alone. There are no objects, just her arousal states. She wants relief. She does not appear to have consistent internal fantasies of drive-gratifying objects that could help her regulate her impulses and provide relief. Often life appears hopeless and vague. At other moments, she fantasizes about being held until her anxiety subsides. This is a step toward development. She is not able to achieve or even entertain a more mature solution: that the environment might need something from her in order to give her the pleasure she seeks.

This patient is furious at those who obtain pleasure. She cannot fathom that they have contributed to this state of affairs: they can love and not just insist on being loved, they can give and not demand in return. This patient exhausts her environment. She wants without giving. Her drive energy goes into self-attack (depression, somatic symptoms, self-destructive choices), periodic outbursts (which drive others further away), and overconsumption, hoarding, collecting, overeating, and excessive drinking.

This patient wishes to experience omnipotent feelings that seem associated with the earliest stages of development. She cannot tolerate feelings of impoverishment and emptiness so tries to incorporate everything. Experiencing constant tension, she can be stilled only by having fantasies of ever-available sources of supply. Since these never materialize, she remains agitated. Nothing fills her. She overconsumes to compensate and feel less anxiety.

Conclusion

Current patterns of overconsumption are multidetermined. Historically, we live in an affluent society where many individuals can be materially well off. This differentiates us from most previous societies. Economist John Galbraith (1998) argues that our society is based on the production of goods that provide employment. Our ideal is of an "expanding economy." Galbraith observed that we became so adept at production that we created an oversupply of goods. "Creating wants" through advertising became the solution to this situation; it was supported by our resolute commitment to an expanding economy. Historian David Potter (1954) posited a motivation behind this ideal: that American character is ingrained with the idea of abundance (being a "people of plenty"). This arose from establishing a country where there seemed to be limitless resources. Once established, resource-consuming patterns appeared natural and right. A comment by George H. W. Bush (qtd. in Kanner & Gomes, 1995), made at the Kyoto Summit in response to criticism about American patterns of overconsumption, reflects this idea: "The American way of life is not up for negotiation" (p. 78). In psychoanalytic terms, overconsumption is ego-syntonic.

Since there is an enormous variance between rich and poor in our country, it is readily apparent that it matters which end of the economic spectrum one falls on (Wachtel, 2002; Schor, 1998). Economic competition makes it difficult to rest on one's laurels. Those who can produce products on a larger scale and more cheaply can drive smaller producers out of business. Fenichel (1938) wrote that because of this system, the "capitalist [must strive for accumulation] under penalty of his own destruction" (p. 72). In understanding overconsumption, then, there is clearly a reciprocal interaction between instinctual impulses and the socioeconomic factors modifying them.

This essay adds the death drive perspective to the discussion. Humans have inherent tendencies to destroy, use up, and seek death.

Harmful overconsumption occurs when psychic structures dominated by destructive instincts succeed in overpowering life-sustaining impulses. A structurally oriented drive theorist would add that impulses are not being held in check by internal psychic mechanisms. Overconsumption also functions as a defense against the awareness of death wishes. Narcissistic fixations keep individuals and groups from maturing to the point of recognizing that they must give to the environment in order to be provided for in a sustainable fashion. Depressive and oedipal dynamics may also explain why specific individuals overconsume.

Individuals need to move beyond the denial of their inherent destructiveness. Psychoanalysts help individuals acknowledge their impulses and the unconscious, omnipotent fantasies associated with them. Analysts explore whether alternative sources of drive satisfaction can be found throughout the process of helping patients put destructive impulses into words. They encourage patients to examine the drive satisfaction they are obtaining: Are they getting the satisfaction they want? What is the satisfaction gained in repeating unsatisfying patterns? As patients move away from narcissism, they learn that they must give in order to receive. Patients introject libidinal objects that will assist in achieving normal drive fusion. An essential ingredient to achieving sustainability is attained—considering the viewpoint of the other that is distinct from, yet inextricably related to, the self. The modern drive perspective complements what other analytic writers have previously identified as the unconscious processes underlying overconsumption: the development of a false consuming self, the repetition of damaged and alienated interpersonal relationships, the culture-wide internalization of an insatiable ego-ideal, the repression of an ecological unconscious, and pathological dissociation from personal suffering so that it has to be projected in order to be experienced. Modern drive theory posits that aggressive instincts, unfused, can manifest in unbridled competition for resources, relentless envy, and total annihilation of the self, the other, and the natural world.

In his essay "Why War?" Freud (1933) put the solution to the predominance of destructive impulses succinctly: Aggressive impulses cannot be disposed of, they can only be diverted. "Anything that encourages the growth of emotional ties between men must operate against war" (p. 284). Environmental exploitation could easily be put in place of war in this argument. Freud saw two means through which emotional ties could be established: by developing loving ties with others and through the process of identification. "Whatever leads men to share important interests produces this community of feeling, these identifications" (p. 212).

Freud's ideas support such interventions as environmental summits where common problems are discussed, and outdoor educational opportunities, where identification with nature is experienced.

Further, drive theory posits that individuals acquire knowledge when they perceive a need to know something (Meadow, personal communication). The need to know depends upon whether drives are being satisfied. For instance, if an individual is in a warm house and can easily pay utility bills, then she may be less concerned about dwindling oil supplies than a person who can no longer pay heating bills, whose needs for security and warmth are threatened. As long as drives are being sated, there will be little need to know about problems and take remedial action. This certainly fits the American pattern of oil overconsumption. Since oil is relatively inexpensive and accessible, many Americans perceive less need to develop the alternative energy strategies evident among nations where prices are higher and local resources are limited.

The neuro-perceptual literature mirrors the modern perspective (Ornstein & Ehrlich, 1989). Humans have inherited modes of thought that are derived from biological and cultural evolution. These automatic ways of processing are tied to the perceptual apparatus. *What we tune into perceptually depends upon our needs.* For example, humans look for discrepancies in the world and respond quickly to sudden shifts, emergencies, and the perception of scarcity. What is close in time and space is immediately overemphasized. Humans also demonstrate a predilection for making simple caricatures instead of thinking probabilistically, analyzing statistics, and recognizing gradual trends.

The pleasure principle proposes that people seek pleasure and avoid pain. It is a central tenet of psychoanalysis and marketing. We might predict, based on it, that individuals would be most likely to consider an alternative course of action if the details of it were laid out for them and the benefits of the strategy were made apparent. Studies demonstrate that consumers are especially persuaded by marketing strategies that communicate how much they are losing by pursuing a costly choice (McKenzie-Mohr & Smith, 1999). People seek to avoid displeasure. One supplier of geothermal heat pumps found an effective way to sell their expensive, alternative heating system. They rent it to customers and take on the burden of maintenance and repair, amortizing the high initial cost of the system over many years. The monthly fee is less than traditional heating costs, so consumers can realize immediate gains. This supplier understands the need to maximize pleasurable elements (inexpensive heat, reasonable solutions, sustainable resources) and minimize unpleasurable dimensions (high initial costs and the hassles of installation and maintenance).

Finally, the public needs to be educated wisely about overconsumption and its effects. For this to be most effective, however, a need for this information must be activated. How can this be done? Individuals become motivated when they think that the cost of an activity is too high, so that its acquisition impedes satisfaction of other needs. They might be informed, for example, of the well-documented research demonstrating that more goods and money do not lead to happiness. They could learn about the unexpected consequences of overconsumption (less time at home because of the hours spent at work, compensatory shopping to cope with resulting states of depletion, less time for relationships, more eating and health-related problems, etc.). This is seldom the message they receive though there is a growing body of professional and popular literature available on this topic (Schor, 1998; Durning, 1995).

Psychoanalysts are well versed in working with individuals who make self-defeating choices. We work regularly with people who resist knowing their unconscious, their repetitions, and the external realities impinging upon them. Because of this, psychoanalysts can shed light on the feelings, fantasies, defenses, and conflicts underlying overconsumption. The voices of psychoanalysis are needed in developing strategies for promoting sustainable consumption.

REFERENCES

Aizenstat, S. (1995), Jungian psychology and the world unconscious. *Ecopsychology: Restoring the Earth, Healing the Mind.* T. Roszak, G. Gomes, & A. Kanner, eds. San Francisco: Sierra Club.

Becker, E. (1997), *The Denial of Death.* New York: Free Press.

Brown, N. (1985), *Life Against Death: The Psychoanalytic Meaning of History.* Middletown, CT: Wesleyan Press.

Chodorow, N. (1978), *The Reproduction of Mothering: Psychoanalysis and the Sociology of Gender.* Berkeley: University of California Press.

Durning, A. (1992), *How Much is Enough? The Consumer Society and the Future of the Earth.* New York: W. W. Norton.

—— (1995), Are we happy yet? *Ecopsychology: Restoring the Earth, Healing the Mind.* T. Roszak, G. Gomes, & A. Kanner, eds. San Francisco: Sierra Club.

Farrell, J. (2003), *One Nation Under Goods.* Washington, DC: Smithsonian Books.

Fechner, Gustav Theodor. (1848) "Ueber das Lustprincip des Handelns." *Zeitschrift fur Philosophie und philosophische Kritik* 19:1–30.

Felch, J. (2003), Concidence theory. *New York Times Magazine.* December 14:60.

Fenichel, O. (1938), The drive to amass wealth. *Psychoanalytic Quarterly,* 7:68–95.

——— (1945), *The Psychoanalytic Theory of Neurosis.* New York: W. W. Norton.

Freud S. (1915–1917), Introductory lectures on psycho-analysis. *Standard Edition.* London: Hogarth Press, 15 & 16.

——— (1920), Beyond the pleasure principle. *Standard Edition.* London: Hogarth Press, 18:13–64.

——— (1923), The ego and the id. *Standard Edition.* London: Hogarth Press, 19:3–64.

——— (1930), Civilization and its discontents. *Standard Edition.* London: Hogarth Press, 21:57–145.

——— (1933), Why war? *Standard Edition.* London: Hogarth Press, 22:197–215.

Galbraith, J. K. (1998), *The Affluent Society.* 40th Anniversary Edition. Boston: Houghton Mifflin.

Gruen, A. (1995), Interview by Derrick Jensen. *Listening to the Land.* D. Jensen, ed. San Francisco: Sierra Club.

Hardin, G. (1968), The tragedy of the commons. *Science,* 162:1243–1248.

Kanner, A. & M. Gomes (1995), The all consuming self. *Ecopsychology: Restoring the Earth, Healing the Mind.* T. Roszak, G. Gomes, & A. Kanner, eds. San Francisco: Sierra Club.

Kaschak, E. (1992), *A New Psychology of Women's Experience.* New York: HarperCollins.

Keepin, W. (2003), Thoughts on psychology and environmental science. *Journal of Psychology and Social Change.* pp. 1–9, www.center-change.org/ejournal/article.

Klein, M., P. Heimann & R. E. Money-Kyrle, eds. (1955), *New Directions in Psycho-analysis: The Significance of Infant Conflict in the Pattern of Adult Behavior.* London: Tavistock.

Kohut, H. (1985), *The Analysis of the Self.* New York: International Universities Press.

Lakoff, G. (2002), *Moral Politics.* Chicago: University of Chicago Press.

Lasch, C. (1979), *The Culture of Narcissism: American Life in an Age of Diminishing Expectations.* New York: W. W. Norton.

Lifton, R. (1976), *Death in Life: Survivors of Hiroshima.* New York: Simon and Schuster.

McKenzie-Mohr, D. & W. Smith. *Fostering Sustainable Behavior: An Introduction to Social Marketing.* Gabriola Island, B.C.: New Society Press.

Meadow, P. W. (2003), *The New Psychoanalysis.* Lanham, MD: Rowman and Littlefield.

Metzner, R. (1993), The split between spirit and nature in european consciousness. *The Trumpter,* 10:1.

Nicholson, S. (2002), *The Love of Nature and the End of the World.* Boston: M.I.T. Press.

Ornstein, R. & P. Ehrlich (1989), *New World, New Mind.* New York: Doubleday.

Pollack, R. (1999), *The Missing Moment: How the Unconscious Shapes Modern Science.* Boston: Houghton Mifflin.

Potter, D. (1954), *People of Plenty: Economic Abundance and the American Character.* Chicago: University of Chicago Press.

Rosenfeld, H. (1971), A clinical approach to the psychoanalytic theory of life and death instincts: an investigation into the aggressive aspects of narcissism. *International Journal of Psychoanalysis,* 52:169–178.

Roszak, T. (1992), *The Voice of the Earth.* New York: Simon & Schuster.

Schmookler, A. (2003), All consuming: materialistic values and human needs. *Journal of Psychology and Social Change.* pp.1–3, www .centerchange.org/ejournal.

Schor, J. (1998), *The Overspect American.* New York: Basic Books.

Searles, H. (1960), *The Nonhuman Environment in Normal Development and in Schizophrenia.* New York: International Universities Press.

———— (1972), Unconscious processes in relation to the environmental crisis. *The Psychoanalytic Review,* 59:361–374.

Shepard, P. (1995). Nature and madness. *Ecopsychology: Restoring the Earth, Healing the Mind.* T. Roszak, G. Gomes, & A. Kanner, eds. San Francisco: Sierra Club.

Silverstein, M. & N. Fiske (2003), *Trading Up The New American Luxury.* New York: Penguin Group.

Solomon, S., J. Greenberg, & T. Pyszczynsk (2003), The fear of death and human destructiveness. *Psychoanalytic Review,* 20:457–474.

Spotnitz, H. (1976), *Psychotherapy of Preoedipal Conditions.* New York: Jason Aronson.

Tarnas, R. (1989), From an archetypal point of view. Paper presented to the conference on "Philosophy and the Human Future." Cambridge, England, August 8.

Velikovski, I. (1982), *Mankind in Amnesia.* Garden City, NY.: Doubleday.

Wachtel, P. (1989), *The Poverty of Affluence.* Philadephia: New Society.

—— (2003), Full pockets, empty lives: a psychoanalytic exploration of the contemporary culture of greed. *American Journal of Psychoanalysis*, 63:103–120.

Wilson, E. (1984), *Biophilia: The Human Bond with Other Species*. Cambridge, MA.: Harvard University Press.

Winnicott, D. (1963), Review of *The NonHuman Environment in Normal Development and Schizophrenia. International Journal of Psychoanalysis*, 44:237–238.

Winter, D. (1996), *Ecological Psychology: Healing the Split Between Planet and Self*. New York: HarperCollins.

—— (2000), Some big ideas for some big problems. *American Psychologist*, 55:516–522.

200 Carlisle Road
Bedford, MA 01730
bigdapeyton@aol.com

Conflict and Deficit in Modern Psychoanalysis

RODRIGO BARAHONA

We'll hunt for a third tiger now, but like
The others this one too will be a form
Of what I dream, a structure of words, and not
The flesh and one tiger that beyond all myths
Paces the earth. I know these things quite well,
Yet nonetheless some force keeps driving me
In this vague, unreasonable, and ancient search,
And I persevere in my quest through time for
Another tiger, the beast not found in verse.

Jorge Luis Borges
Para ti, Lucia

Is modern psychoanalysis only a theory of technique? In a critique and defense of modern psychoanalysis, the author describes what he views as the primary epistemological difficulties in modern psychoanalytic theory, vis-a-vis the greater psychoanalytic community, that may be contributing to an "existential crisis" in its theory and theorists. Drawing from the work of other psychoanalytic traditions, the author argues that far from being just a theory of technique and, therefore, lacking as far as mind theory, modern psychoanalysis is embedded in traditional and contemporary theory, theoretical introjects of a sort, whether this is formally recognized or not. For example, the author describes how, in his view, Spotnitz and Meadow's conception of the development and workings of the early infantile psyche and of pathology can be alternatively understood as a theory of internal object relations, indeed, that a theory of internal object relations is implicit in their work. From this perspective, the author attempts to clarify what in modern analytic literature could be described as the "killing off" or the "death" of the object in narcissism and, more specifically, schizophrenia and concludes that in both of these states the object is never truly dead.

Modern psychoanalysis is in a state of existential crisis. At least this is what some students and analysts from modern analytic institutes seem to think. The recent visit of Dany Nobus to the Boston Graduate School of Psychoanalysis (BGSP) and the Center for Modern Psychoanalytic Studies (CMPS) has had many people wondering how and why Lacanian analysis is being introduced into modern psychoanalytic thinking. Is there a need to import Lacanian concepts into modern psychoanalysis? If so, what does that say about modern psychoanalytic theory itself?

Modern Psychoanalysis: Only a Theory of Technique?

It has become increasingly common to hear respected figures in modern psychoanalysis claim in classrooms and other psychoanalytic circles that modern psychoanalysis is only a theory of technique, implying that it lacks a theory of mind. This is a perspective that I too, coming from a background heavily rooted in the Lacanian tradition, have many times held. But can this be true? After a careful reading of *Modern Psychoanalysis of the Schizophrenic Patient* (Spotnitz, 2004), *Psychotherapy of Preoedipal Conditions* (Spotnitz, 1987), and *Treatment of the Narcissistic Neuroses* (Spotnitz & Meadow, 1999)— can one still claim that an attempt at a modern psychoanalytic theory of mind has not been made by at least Spotnitz and Meadow? If we consider the *Selected Papers of Phyllis W. Meadow*, published in *Modern Psychoanalysis* (1996c), as constituting the fourth book in the modern analytic series, would not the considerate and careful reader of the whole series be able to point out a major, though subtle, epistemological shift that has occurred between Spotnitz's first book (originally 1969; cited here in its 2004 second edition) and Meadow's of 1996? How many students, especially those coming from backgrounds within different traditions in psychoanalysis, have reflected on how Meadow's insistent drive and fantasy focus is sometimes at great odds with certain aspects of Spotnitz's work that seem to suggest an object relations perspective? Can we even talk about epistemological shifts in theories of mind that some modern analysts are now claiming do not exist in modern psychoanalysis?

Separating from the Other

To be sure, there is a modern psychoanalytic theory of mind, as con-flicted and epistemologically inconsistent as it may at times appear to be. Some authors, Kirman (1998) and Marshall (1998) standing out among them, have gone to great lengths to locate modern psychoanaly-sis within an understandable paradigm in relation to other schools of thought. Kirman locates the modern school somewhere between a one-person and a two-person psychology. Representing the former in its extreme form is the classical school, probably closer to the ego psy-chology of the Hartmann era. Representing the latter extreme are the relationist schools, the intersubjectivists and the post-modern traditions of psychoanalysis, best represented by the works of Ogden, Mitchell, Benjamin, and Hoffman, among many others. Indeed, the psychoana-lytic pendulum seems to be swinging more and more toward the rela-tionist perspective, and with good reason. The relationists embrace ideas from almost every other school of thought in psychoanalysis, from Lacan to Kohut, as all of them have in common a rejection of ego psychology. Modern psychoanalysis started out this very same way— embracing most of Freud's basic concepts, most notably his controver-sial dual drive theory, but offering an alternative form of treatment for narcissism that, to modern analysts, provided an escape from the restrictive and sometimes excessively rigid practice of classical analy-sis. It is no wonder then that many students of modern psychoanalysis embrace, for example, Ogden's (1982) somewhat relationist conceptu-alization of the clinical and theoretical implications of projective iden-tification because it seems to describe so well what in modern psycho-analytic circles is known as emotional induction, but without the semantic confusions provided by the many different readings and mis-readings of the concept of *object* (which I will discuss in detail below) that is inherent in projective identification but not in emotional induc-tion. This is so because, as Kirman (1998) points out, it is clear that there is much in the two-person position that can be endorsed by mod-ern analysts, such as the belief that the impersonal analyst is a myth (Meadow, 1996b) and that psychoanalysis is therapeutic due more to the emotional engagement between patient and analyst than to "true" interpretations. It should be noted, however, that this does not mean that two-person psychoanalysts, i.e., relationists, do not use interpretations; in fact they rely heavily on them. The difference is that, within the theoretical context of relational theory, the act of interpreting has its value as a relational event aimed at making personal experience more real and meaningful, rather than making the unconscious conscious. (See Mitchell [1981] for a tour through relational perspectives compared to other psychoanalytic theories.)

In fact, Kirman (1998) states, "a sampling of modern analytic interactions might very well turn up not only interpretations, but self-disclosures and emotional communications of countertransference" (p. 20). He is quick to clarify, however, that a modern analyst would have a different aim in mind when intervening in these manners. That is, a relationist might intervene using countertransference feelings to convey a sense of mutuality, of authenticity that will contribute to the patient's growing sense of authenticity (because it was once lacking), his sense of being alive; the same intervention in the hands of a modern analyst might be employed with the intent of focusing on the transference and resolving a specific resistance. Of course, we are not just talking about different types of analysts, but of different types of patients as well. The patient of the relationist is one whose mind is viewed as having developed out of meaningful interactional configurations of the self in relation to others. This contributes to the establishment or pathology of *self-authenticity*—the feeling that one is real and alive and the subject of one's own discourse—an idea that is very close to the Lacanian theme of subjectification in analysis. The modern psychoanalytic patient can be conceptualized through the lens of traditional drive theory—mind and pathology are the product of conflict and compromise between libidinal and aggressive drives, and the defenses erected against them. Another way to put it is to say that the former is a meaning-generating animal while the latter is a drive-regulated animal (Greenberg & Mitchell, 1983).

It is important for us as modern analysts at a time of "existential crisis" to take heed of the nuances pointed out by Kirman and Mitchell among competing theories in psychoanalysis since, as we know, by setting ourselves apart from the other we establish our own sense of who we are. Yes, indeed, modern psychoanalysis has a mind theory although it appears to me that it is one that has not been transmitted clearly enough from one generation to the next, due probably to many factors, some of which are discussed below. The future of our theory relies on a careful delineation and reconstruction of the basic assumptions of modern analysis that we can agree still hold true, and then the *mindful* and *selec-*

tive importation of useful and important concepts from other traditions in psychoanalysis that can further our own style of analytical thinking. This means an acute awareness of the sometimes subtle, yet significant, gaps between psychoanalytic epistemologies.

For example, at the first of a series of lectures given by Dany Nobus at BGSP and CMPS, respectively, early in the Spring of 2002, one modern analyst expressed, to the agreement of many others present, that a specific Lacanian intervention being presented was identical to one that modern analysts perform regularly. This intervention was the analyst's repetition of a phrase that the patient had just uttered. The modern analyst pronounced that "we do the same thing" and, in the euphoria of the moment, a marriage between the two theories was practically in the works. However, a careful reading of the situation reveals that the two interventions are actually antithetical because of the completely different theoretical context in which they make sense, which of course implies entirely different aims.

The Lacanian analyst "punctuates" (Lacan, 1977) to indicate that there is something there in what the patient has just said onto which his (the patient's) attention might be better focused. The analyst is sensing a space in which a possible "opening up of the unconscious" is happening. It is a space for rational introspection on the part of the patient. The analyst's utterance is an enigma for the patient to now attempt to figure out:

> Just as the meaning of a written text can often be changed by changing the punctuation (commas, dashes, periods) the patient's own punctuation of his or her speech—emphasizing ("underlining") certain words, glossing rapidly over mistakes or slurs, repeating what he or she thinks is important—can be modified, the analyst suggesting through his or her own punctuation that another reading is possible, but without saying what it is or even that it is clear and coherent. By emphasizing ambiguities, double entendres, and slips, the analyst does not so much convey that he or she knows what the patient "really meant" as hint that other meanings, perhaps revealing meanings, are possible. The analyst's punctuation does not so much point to or nail down one particular meaning as suggest a level of meanings the patient has not been attentive to: unintended meanings, unconscious meanings. (Fink, 1997, p. 12)

In the psychical landscape of the analysand, the analyst has appeared as an other, or rather as a symbolic *O*ther. This suggests that a level of "unknown" is placed between the subject and the Other—they are essentially different. On the other hand, for the modern analyst, the "reflection" of what the patient has said could mean that the analyst has perceived the patient's question as a resistance and is therefore applying his utterance to that *as a resistance*. The intervention is designed to introduce the analyst into the psychical landscape of the patient in an ego-syntonic or dystonic way. What's more, it is designed so that, for the patient, the analyst represents a narcissistic reflection of himself. He is unchallenged in his use of defensive structure; a space allowing for therapeutic regression is opened up; a narcissistic transference, one of the initial aims and vehicles of modern analytic treatment, is fostered. But here, from the Lacanian perspective, the modern analyst is allowing himself to be molded in the image of the patient's narcissistic projections and is for the patient not the Other, but the other. That is, not the symbolic Other, but an imaginary other—a position to be avoided by the analyst in Lacanian theory as it reflects an elaboration of the patient's ego which defensively cements the analyst in the imaginary position of the *subject supposed to know*. Which is not to say that the imaginary does not have an important place in Lacanian clinical theory in regards to technique— that is, it is not simply ignored. The difference lies in the fact that for moderns, the analyst enters the imaginary (the narcissistic) deliberately, not only by allowing himself to be situated there through the patient's transference but also by the active interventions of the analyst (such as mirroring and joining), timed to the transference, with the aim of working through to the symbolic. By no means does the experienced modern analyst make the mistake of assuming that in the narcissistic-imaginary field the patient has the capacity to symbolize. However, as is clearer in Lacan's early work on technique, the Lacanian analyst, while allowing for these imaginary identifications to take place, does not actively encourage or reinforce them through interventions designed for that purpose. As Fink (1997) tells us:

> [T]o emphasize the symbolic is to diminish the importance of the imaginary. If, however, the analyst allows him- or herself to be cast in the role of someone like the analysand (an imaginary other as opposed to the symbolic Other), it is the analyst's ego that becomes situated at one end of the imaginary axis in juxtaposition to the analysand's ego, and the analysis bogs down in rivalrous power struggles and identifications. By falling into the trap of the imaginary identifications, the analyst loses sight of the symbolic dimension—"the only dimension that cures," as Lacan says. (p. 35)

Although, for both moderns and Lacanians, the final aim of analysis is to "pierce through the imaginary dimension which veils the symbolic" (p. 35), the immediate aims of the analyst (that is, the purpose of the specific intervention) are different, as can be seen in the case of the intervention discussed above. By uttering the same words to the patient at the same time, the modern analyst and the Lacanian are doing two entirely different things. Because, however, as I will explain further below, the modern analyst works with the narcissistic elements of the patient's pathology across different diagnostic categories and in this way views pathology as functioning on a spectrum, it would appear to make clinical sense for the modern analyst to work in this way. For the Lacanian, however, there is no spectrum, and pathology is situated in three conceptually stable, if clinically unstable, diagnostic categories. Therefore, it seems to me, it would make sense for the Lacanian to work only with psychotics in the way that moderns work across pathologies while at the same time maintaining a sensitivity to the differences from case to case (Meadow, 1999).

Modern Psychoanalysis: A Relational Perspective?

Interestingly, Kirman (1998) does not define modern psychoanalysis as either a one-person or two-person psychology. He is clear in separating modern theory (of technique) from what he very diplomatically portrays as the rigidity of one-person theories as well as from the at times excessive relationist and constructivist approaches of two-person models. Modern psychoanalysis, one would gather from his article, is somewhere in between. This point is taken up by Marshall (1998) when he suggests that Spotnitz's work represents an integration of the two-person model and the intrapsychic focus.

It becomes even more complicated when attempting to make sense out of the interrelation between our *clinical* and *mind* theory along the lines of the two other almost parallel psychoanalytic paradigms: the drive (intrapsychic conflict) model and relational (developmental defect and deficit) model. Some have argued that these two paradigms represent a false dichotomy (Eagle, 1984) or at least an oversimplification (Richards, 1999). Nevertheless, they exist and provide useful guidelines for tracing the roots and limitations of one's psychoanalytic theory. A careful reading of Greenberg and Mitchell's (1983) book, where these paradigms make a carefully elucidated appearance, reveals that modern psychoanalysis as a theory of *mind* fits perfectly well into one paradigm (at least the Meadovian trends in modern theory) while as a theory of *technique* it can only be justified through the lens of its competition. Obviously, a more detailed study of this is warranted before drawing any definite conclusions on the epistemological status of the modern theory of mind if, in fact, and contrary to rumor, it exists at all. But I'd like to attempt, before going any further, to consider some of the less subtle discrepancies that as a student and practitioner I have often wondered about. It seems to me that the modern psychoanalytic theory of the mind, derived as it is from basic Freudian drive theory, postulates mind as constituted out of intrapsychic conflict, with a special emphasis on the constructive and destructive effects of the fusion and defusion of the life and death drives in pathology and in so-called normal psychic life. Thus, theoretically, modern analytic theory finds itself perfectly capable of filling a slot in a paradigm that paradoxically, according to the principles drawn up by Greenberg and Mitchell, necessitates a theory of technique that some modern analysts repudiate. As some practitioners understand it, as drive theorists, modern analysts reject the techniques of interpretation and the position of the blank-screen analyst, techniques derived from the basic tenets of drive theory itself with its primary emphasis on the patient's drives in the fantasy life of the analysand. At best, modern analysts admit to the usefulness of interpretations, rejecting, however, the heavy reliance on them as the sine qua non of analytic technique in favor of the powerful intervention of emotional communication—which brings me to the next discrepancy.

At the other end of this paradigmatic dilemma is this: When emphasizing the importance of the analyst's use of countertransference as an analytic tool for not just gauging the patient's drive states during the session but also as fuel for emotional communications, the modern analyst, it could be said, is unwittingly entering the territory of the second paradigm, that of the relational or deficit model. Now there is not just one set of drives but rather two in the session, the patient's and the analyst's. Even if the patient is not aware of the analyst's countertransference, in relationist terms we are dealing with two subjectivities—not just the inevitable and often accidental subjectivity of the analyst, but his intentional subjectivity: the analyst's countertransference, objective and subjective, as an analytic tool. The point can be made from the modern analytic perspective that, in a sense, there is still only one subjectivity at play here, and that the analyst finds within himself that which already belongs to the patient but has been split off. In fact, to the question of whether or not modern psychoanalysis would not be more coherently viewed as a two-person psychology, Meadow states that "one would practically have to be blind to believe there is only one person in the room during treatment, or that each person, analysand and analyst, doesn't possess his own set of drives, desires, and defenses" (Meadow, personal communication). She goes on to explain that there are always two biological entities present in the analytic situation, and that the reason the psychoanalytic training process is so lengthy is so that one person, defined as the patient, can be the focus of these two biological entities. The analyst's internal states, in turn, can be studied and confirmed in his own supervision or analysis. What's more, the awareness that the analyst's drives are not so different from those of the patient results from the analyst's availability to be induced with the patient's internal states—a byproduct of his comfort with his own drive states. From the modern point of view, then, "there is one person in the room undergoing treatment and all forces are, in a successful analysis, concentrated on the resolution of conflict in the one—not two" (Meadow, personal communication).

But how does one reconcile this position, as a one-person-psychology position, with the modern analytic literature emphasizing the use of the analyst's countertransference as an analytic tool, and not merely something to be discarded as an obfuscation of the patient's transference? As Meadow explained in some comments to an early draft of this paper, the analyst reaches into himself to find his own drives exaggerated in the pathology of the patient. But, does this not lead to a further intersubjective understanding of the analytic process, that is, to the idea that the subjective experience of the analyst can be magnified (subjective countertransference) if not transformed (objective countertransference) by the subjectivity of the other, and vice versa? In the simplest terms, would effective analysis be possible if not for the real effects that each participant has on the phantasy life of the other? As Meadow (1999) writes, "the concept of joining, even exaggerating a patient's disguised feelings, is based on feelings genuinely experienced by the analyst" (p. 34). In delivering an emotional communication, the modern analyst does not merely *imitate* a response that he would consider maturational for the patient, or that the patient fantasizes was lacking in his panoply of maturational life experiences; rather he waits until that response is stirred in him, and then delivers it with an authenticity that makes it effective.

Nowhere is this more evident than in the new and promising idea of the *anaclitic countertransference*, an idea that has nevertheless remained controversial among modern analysts. Liegner (1995) defines this as a point in the analysis, presumably after much has already been worked through, where feelings of the patient "turn out to be the very feelings *of which the patient was deprived* during his dependent years, yet which were needed for his maturation" (p. 154, italics added). Liegner goes on to explain that "these feelings come about as a product of the relationship" (p. 154). A comment by Spotnitz (quoted in Liegner, 1995, pp. 162–163) claiming that "the use of the anaclitic countertransference can repair emotional deficiencies resulting from family genes, defective fetal environment, or infantile trauma" further describes the therapeutic interaction as one of repairing structural deficits resulting from environmental failures. Liegner (1995) observes her use of the anaclitic countertransference in the case of Jacob. It is important to note that what she is calling here an *interpretation* is provided in the form of an *emotional communication*.

> A vague stirring within me had grown in intensity in my determination to "bring him to life." Gradually his frozen exterior began to thaw as this new feeling led to greater affective verbal activity on my part. With the knowledge of his history, I also gave him the interpretation that he had not been allowed to have any emotions but that I wanted to hear and know them. He wept for the first time. (pp. 155–156)

This is about as good a fit as you will ever find to the relational model, where the patient suffers from deprivation and lack, rather than conflict, and the analytic function consists in providing him with the emotional experience that he needs to help him back on the developmental track. It's true that there may be another possible way of understanding this above dynamic, i.e., that the conflict is unconscious, and in between revealing feelings (being known) and being loved (the unknown), the lack in this case is there, but the problem is the patient's inability to solve it with others due to conflict (Meadow, personal communication). Still, it appears to me that even if one wished to view these "deficits" as caused by conflicts, that is, that the patient's drive conflicts are what caused him to perceive the world as having failed him (in phantasy), the analyst's response here is as therapeutic as it is environmental. I think Hurevitch (1999) was correct in drawing parallels between the anaclitic countertransference and Winnicott's (1965) *holding environment* or Alexander and French's infamous *corrective emotional experience*. Yet this technique, which consists of the patient receiving a feeling out of interaction with his environment (the analyst), stems from a modern analytic theory of mind which pays little or no attention to the impact of the environment on the emerging psyche.

* * *

> I think that psychoanalysis is about nothing more than accepting our limits which involve the Other, our neighbor, who is different . . . [T]his is

only possible if the intersection between the two is limited in such a way
that each person remains himself while being with the other. Being either
completely the One or completely the Other is impossible.

André Green, Life Narcissism, Death Narcissism

Integration

In this paper I have attempted to point out just a few of the conflicts and
deficits that I have perceived as having contributed to the existential
crisis of modern psychoanalysis. As stated earlier, it is well known that
an important part of defining one's own sense of self comes from differentiation from the Other, and Kirman's and Marshall's papers go a
long way toward doing just that, the latter between Spotnitzian analysis
and Kohutian self-psychology. Defining what one isn't defines one's
own theory, be it a loose group of theoretical assumptions or a whole,
consistent system. But a tremendous mistake is made when we, in the
spirit of separating ourselves from the Other, refuse to acknowledge—
that is, deny, split, or project—the part of the Other that remains in us.
It is as if we believed ourselves to be a product of spontaneous generation, forgetting that the theoretical Name-of-the-Father in the process of
separating us from the Other at once marks our place among generations of theories that, like aging parents, are still our living contempo-
raries. From here stem the unhelpful myths, certainly not represented
by all modern analysts, that we discovered countertransference, were
the first to work successfully with psychosis, and discovered the
destructive effects of aggression on the mind—claims that sadly ignore
the work of analysts outside of New York City, like Racker, Klein,
Winnicott, Aulagnier, Bion, and Lacan, to name only a few of the
principals—ignoring the work of these theorists and clinicians because
they are object relationists, anything other than pure drive theorists, or
they are just too "classical," especially in light of the modern analytic
paradigm conflict. This can only contribute to the feeling that we
indeed do not have a *mind theory* since, in our work, many times the
only references we seem to find are to ourselves.

The example that I would now like to put forward serves as an illustration of what I have proposed here in the previous paragraph. I take
issue specifically with the modern psychoanalytic concept of *object*. It
is my belief that this concept has been regrettably misunderstood in
modern analysis in such a way that it has contributed to our self-

isolation from, rather than our inclusion in, the broader corpus of contemporary psychoanalysis. This in turn has contributed to the idea that modern psychoanalysis has no theory of mind. I would like to now briefly discuss the use of the concept of *object* in modern analytic literature, specifically in discussions on the narcissistic defense and Spotnitz's theories of the ego and object fields of the mind.

The Narcissistic Defense and the Modern Analytic Death of the Object

When frustration-aggression is mobilized in the narcissistic patient, it remains concentrated on the self rather than discharged onto the object that the individual subjectively perceives to be the cause of the unpleasurable affective states. Rather than this aggression being vented on the external object, the aggression targets the infant's emerging internal self- and object-representations, located in the object and ego fields of the mind (Spotnitz, 1999, p. 57), what in modern analytic discourse has often been referred to as the *destruction* or the *killing off* of the object. This is done, paradoxically, in the service of object protection. The object is protected, as will be explained more fully below, because it is felt to be needed by the person. So if the object is protected, how come modern analysts talk about the schizophrenic, for example, as not having any objects? How does one not have an object, kill it off, and protect it at the same time?

To understand this more fully, it is necessary to explain what is meant by object and ego fields of the mind. Spotnitz (1999) described the emerging psyche as divided into two parts, the ego and the object fields. The object field develops first; in it are recorded "impressions of the infant's own bodily sensations as well as those of his mother's ministrations during his first few months of life" (p. 159). So, all of the sensations, internally or externally derived, become initially represented in what he calls the first object field of the mind. These internally and externally derived sensations are meshed with one another and the infant still "has no sense of separateness from the external world" (p. 159). So far, Spotnitz's conception of the object field is that it is made up of *impressions* or *sensations*. He goes on to say that the ego field, which will contain the representations or impressions (as Spotnitz uses the two concepts interchangeably) of internal and external stimuli that will become associated with the self, emerges from the first object field: "With the quantitative sorting out of the impressions of the self, a part of the object field becomes the ego field" (Spotnitz, 1999, p. 159).

Spotnitz does not explain exactly how this happens, but as development continues, soon the individual has a set of self-representations in the ego field and object-representations in the object field of the mind. In narcissistic disorders like schizophrenia, Spotnitz (1999) says that:

> *Objects* previously established in the object field of the mind are talked about as though they are a part of the ego; object patterns that moved into the ego field early in life (identifications) are referred to as though they are in the object field. (p. 160, italics added)

This passage suggests that the schizophrenic has internal objects, that is, a set of object-representations and a set of self-representations. (A more in-depth discussion of this can be found below; it is important to note that in the modern view, these self-representations and object-representations would be viewed as internal responses to stimulation from the outside, not resembling or incarnating actual objects.) However, under the pressure of mobilized aggression, he regresses back to a state where there is no differentiation between the two sets, so that what would ordinarily be felt as an attack from an outside external object (whether real or imagined) does not register and become stored in a separate object field but rather is confused with the self-representations of the ego field. External frustrating and therefore *bad* objects, rather than making separate impressions on the object field, are confused by the patient for *bad* self-representations. Spotnitz calls this "egotization of the object" (p. 160). Because of egotization of the object, the attack now comes from the inside.

Egotization, to my mind (I won't speak for Spotnitz or Meadow), is one of the initial steps toward (external and internal) object protection. The boundaries between self and object become blurred *defensively* so that it is not the external object that is bad, but rather the self that is undeserving. (It is probably important to emphasize here that when Spotnitz and Meadow talk about an "external object," they are usually referring to the individual's internal fantasy of the object, usually centering around affective states experienced in relation to this object, transposed or projected onto its outside representative. Meadow's famous statement "There's no such thing as a mother" is an example of this. "He [the child] would rather believe that he is undeserving of the mother's love than that she is emotionally defective" [Spotnitz & Meadow, 1995, p. 46].)

This then is what constitutes object protection in schizophrenia. Spotnitz and Meadow (1995) describe a three-step process: 1) aggression against mental functioning, 2) protection of the object field of the mind, and 3) sacrifice of the self.

I would like to describe in detail how these processes occur in schizophrenia. First, the external object is at some level perceived as bad, and second, the ego denies itself this perception and instead wipes out the internal representation of the external object (what is meant by "there is no object") so as to assure that it will not remain a stimulating presence in the psyche. If the stimulation continues and the impulses that arise from within continue to push for discharge, then the aggression is directed against the ego's perceptual and executive capacities in the form of distortions or a reworking of the internal perception of external events—essentially an attack on the individual's thought process so as not to be compelled to act aggressively on the perceived (real or fantasized) external danger. This is essentially Freud's (1911) description of the delusional process in paranoid schizophrenia, as he outlined in the Schreber case, in the sense that a new reality is constructed in the place of the old, frustrating one of the real world. We can assume then that a *delusional system of internal object relations* has set in; this is evidence that libidinal re-cathexis of phantasy objects may also be at work in schizophrenia in an effort to rebuild what it is constantly destroying. In Green's (1999) terminology, a process of objectalization has set in to counter the equally powerful push for de-objectalization in the service of the death drive.

Both of these processes, libidinal and aggressive, entail a defensive confusing of object-representations with self-representations. The sacrifice of the self comes, I assume, from what must be a now deadened internal landscape where all possibility of real and meaningful self-experience has been annihilated through the further destruction of self-representations (made up of egotized objects) and their substitution for what could be called *delusional object relations*—object relations nevertheless as opposed to just internal fantasized object relations, which in substance amount to the same thing but differ as far as their reason for being. The latter represents an attempt to represent drive states in a way that is manageable to the ego, and in this sense there is a direct correspondence between tension states and the constitution of the internal objects. In delusional object relations, as seen in paranoia, the same process takes place—only there is a further aim in addition to the sorting out of tension states—the construction of a vision of the world that makes sense to the subject in place of the void caused by the destruction of his original world view. Thus, *delusional object relations* essentially involve a re-working of the meanings derived from brushes with the world outside juxtaposed with internal tension states in a way that has to do more with coherence than correspondence.

Again, while external object relations are maintained through the narcissistic defense (picture the deluded schizophrenic in the middle of a crowded park), internal object relations are attacked as the aggression becomes concentrated on destroying and/or transforming object impressions and the thought process. However, I would argue that it is incorrect to say that the schizophrenic always has no objects because the narcissistic defense, as described above, is mobilized only after the object is first perceived as bad. Also, as I just described, the schizophrenic through his delusion *maintains* his relation to his objects, facilitated as it may be by phantasy. Spotnitz's concept of regression and the wiping out of the boundary between object and self fields of the mind suggests that the schizophrenic is not always in this state of "objectlessness." He has established some self- and object-representations, and only mixes and destroys them under the stress of psychic pain. I would even say that the schizophrenic never destroys them, but rather is in a constant state of destroying them. Internal objects are never wiped out but are always, as in the case of the schizophrenic in crisis, under attack. The idea that a defense is in place implies intuitively that threatening objects still loom about.

In any case, Spotnitz and Meadow (1995, p. 49) explain that in another narcissistic disorder, depression, the internal object-representations are not so much wiped out as they are confused with the self-representations so that the meanings and "bad" feelings associated with the disappointing object become attached to the self, now experienced as bad and hateful (i.e., the projected parts which created the object field are taken back into the self). So, instead of a fundamental breakdown of the thinking process, it shares with paranoia a distortion in the meaning-making process (that which attaches values to things) so that the meaning gotten out of the self's interactions with its object is transformed essentially into the self's interaction with itself: *I hate you because you left me* becomes *I hate myself for making you leave me.* This process is as narcissistic as it is internally relational.

Again, this is by definition a narcissistic system where meanings and perceptions are partially internally generated and partially based on realistic exchanges with the external environment. The realistic exchange with the object, e.g., a frustrating mother object experience, becomes subjectively owned by the self and is another example of defensive egotization. As such, a mother whom the child perceives as not meeting his needs is preserved as a good mother while the corresponding bad representation of the incompetent mother is defensively confused with the self. This assures that the tie between infant and mother is maintained, even if only for the pleasurable experiences the mother provides. Aggression is bound by libido within the system of self-representations in the now meshed ego-object field and not discharged externally.

A Brief Note on the Concept of Narcissism

It may be at this point in the paper helpful to distinguish narcissism as a *disorder* from narcissism as a *vicissitude* of the drive. In case discussions, for example, one sometimes gets the impression that narcissism and psychosis are equivalent, and that most if not all of the patients discussed are "object-less" psychotics. "The patient is not at that level yet" is frequently heard at the mere mention of the patient's mother. This unusual phenomenon that as modern analysts we seem to be psychosis-magnets unfortunately contributes, I think, to the oedipus complex phobia that in my opinion opens an enormous vacuum in our patients. It seems that *narcissism* should not be presented as a diagnostic category in itself (our *narcissism* is entirely self-involved and has nothing to do with the well-established *"Narcissistic Personality Disorder"* generally excepted in most schools of analysis) but as a vicissitude of the drive leading to a more or less fixed mental state within one or many different diagnostic types. Thus, modern analytic technique is designed to treat the narcissistic elements of every disorder, inherent in all levels of pathology, even neurosis, and not just reserved for the mythical "narcissist."

The Nature of the Object in Spotnitz and Meadow

It is often unclear to the beginning, and even the experienced, student of modern psychoanalysis what, modern analytically, constitutes an *object*. In modern psychoanalytic literature, concepts like "impressions," "object "representations," and "objects" are used interchangeably. When discussing cases in class discussions, students use the word "object" to mean whole, oedipal object, and, thus preoedipal is synonymous with pre-object. What does the object field of the mind, which is clearly developed very early in life, contain? Objects? Internal objects (which in analytic literature are identical with the concept of object-representations)? Impressions? Sensations? Spotnitz and Meadow hardly write about internal object relations, but rather use the term "object-representations," referring to what sometimes seems to be the mnemic trace of the affective experience of the infant in regards to internal and external stimuli. This is sometimes unclear even within the main modern psychoanalytic texts by Spotnitz (1999) and Spotnitz and Meadow (1995), as can be seen in this passage: "Impressions made on the object field, *object-representations*, are *egotized*; that is, they are misidentified as experiences of the ego field. *The patient may refer to feelings that he originally experiences from a significant early object as his own feelings*" (Spotnitz, 1999, p. 160) (first two italics added).

Let's say that the contents of the ego and object fields of the mind are object-representations, and therefore, according to the other schools of psychoanalytic thought, internal objects. Are these *internally generated* internal objects, constituted primarily from the energy of the drives, libidinal and aggressive, and like Winnicott's "subjective objects" (Ogden, 1990, p. 173), based on internal phantasy alone? Or are they a reflection of realistic encounters with external objects? The italicized sentence in the passage cited above reflects some of this ambiguity. Are these feelings that the patient projected on to the object, i.e., a frustrated patient creates a frustrating object, or are they the object's feelings taken by the patient to be his own, i.e., an anxious object creates an anxious patient? This speaks to the fundamental question of nature versus nurture. Are our internal worlds generated from our internal needs regardless of our surrounding reality or do impressions of our external reality become the first occupants of our internal worlds?

Take another passage from Spotnitz and Meadow (1995) on the mother:

> Whether she actually loved the infant, hated him, or was indifferent to him is less significant than the fact that the totality of his experience [not environment] failed to meet his specific emotional needs and caused him to perceive his environment on the whole as an extremely frustrating one. (p. 45)

This passage is crucial in understanding what I think is the evolving perspective of modern psychoanalysis on this matter, and possibly a difference between the ideas contained in *Modern Psychoanalysis of the Schizophrenic Patient* (2004 [1976]) (where the object is more or less portrayed as primarily introjected) and the more recent *Treatment of the Narcissistic Neuroses* (1995) in which this passage is found (where the object is projected onto the object field and sometimes externalized). The emphasis here on the child's experience of the environment rather than on the actions of the environment on the child points to an internal object world generated under the pressure of impulses, aggressive and libidinal, and the affect states associated with them at different moments. This represents, of course, a truly Freudian depiction of drive theory in its extreme, where there is no inherent object, no preordained tie to the human environment. The object is "created" by the individual out of the experiences of drive satisfaction and frustration (Greenberg & Mitchell, 1983). Spotnitz and Meadow are not denying here the impact of the environment; *it is just not their object of study*, so to speak. For them, as for most drive theorists, it is the individual's perception and therefore processing of the experience that is psychologically enhancing or destructive. For these clinicians, this is the object of psychoanalytic investigation. The crucial difference between modern psychoanalytic drive theory, then, and the most relational of the object relations theories (not represented by Melanie Klein) is that for Spotnitz and Meadow the psyche seeks to repeat experiences with objects for the affective releases that these bring, whereas for relational theorists (like Fairbairn and Guntrip) the psyche seeks contact with objects, and the affective experience is just one way of contact. Modern psychoanalysts, as drive theorists, conceive of a mind that seeks pleasure and seeks to reduce unpleasure with or without the object. Where "social ties are secondary, they are contingent upon the ability of other people to facilitate the discharge of drive-derived needs" (Greenberg & Mitchell, 1983, p. 46). This view, the reader will note, is a simplification of Freud's (1930) basic thesis best described in his monumental "Civilization and its Discontents" where he describes society and social relations as essentially drive derivatives created under pressure for the discharge and simultaneous control of and over the drives. The relational theorist's conception of mind attains pleasure *because* of its social relations or, in other words, its relation to objects.

So what is it that inhabits the mind of the early infant? Objects or pre-object fantasies? Sensations? I think both—to my mind they are one and the same thing psychoanalytically (phenomenologically), different only in terms of schools of thought. Consider this passage from Meadow (1996a):

> The first rumblings of the wish to live, seen in the strivings for an object world, can now be viewed as a search for an external port for impulse discharge. Early perceptions of that world reflect the internal balance between

constructive and destructive forces. Images, as the first constructions of the ego, are not a new concept in analysis. Freud wrote of the role of hallucination in the infant's search for gratification. How we use images may have changed. If the infant needs a supply of milk he may call up a fountain. If he is frustrated and enraged he may call up a demon. (p. 160)

The first part of this excerpt suggests that for the author, the object world is the equivalent of an external port. Is there a place, in modern theory, for an internal object world before the recognition of whole external objects? Can there be, as in Klein's theory, internal fantasized objects to contain the balance of the infantile psyche's discharging drives? The fountains and demons Meadow writes about are referred to as images, and as they are conjured up by the infantile psyche, they are representatives of the drives.

Now consider this passage from Greenberg and Mitchell (1983) on Winnicott's (1965) "moment of illusion" concept:

In addition to "holding," the mother "brings the world to the child" and, in Winnicott's view, this function plays a crucial and intricate role in development. The infant when excited conjures up, or, more precisely, is on the verge of conjuring up, an object suitable to his needs. Ideally it is precisely at that moment that the devoted mother presents him with such a suitable object—the breast for example. This is the "moment of illusion." The infant believes he has created the object. Over and over the infant hallucinates, the mother presents, and the content of the conjuring approximates more and more closely to the real world. (p. 192)

In both of these passages, Meadow's and Greenberg and Mitchell's, the words *object* and *images* could be interchanged without altering the meaning of the intrapsychic phenomenon being described. Clearly, the difference in terms comes not from the nature of the phenomenon but from differences in the languages of two compatible, yet separate, schools of thought.

A Theory of Internal Objects within Modern Psychoanalysis.

What is it that occurs when this separation between ego and object fields of the mind happens? To my mind, this is best conceptualized in the following terms: What are registered in the first object field are impressions of affect states in relation, as Spotnitz (1999) describes, to internal and external sensations. These impressions *are the first internal objects* and have probably been there since the beginning of the infant's existence. They have existed in a way that may not have as yet *meant* anything to the infant's still underdeveloped psyche, but nevertheless have affected the internal balance and economy of the drives in the unconscious.

These affect states and internal/external sensations are not yet distinguishable from one another. As the child continues to develop, but still very early on in psychic life, his concept of the affective state in this first object field gradually becomes separated into a growing awareness of "something causing something to something else." Out of this initial affective state, which constitutes the first object field of the mind, then, grows the first self-representation (which moves into and forms the ego field) and the first *separate* object-representations (which remain in the object field). The affect state from which these two are derived becomes the link between them. Thus is constituted the first *internal* object relation. There is now an affective link between the new object field and the new ego field.

In other words, the first object field, constituted by affective representations, has turned into two separate representational fields with the affective link in between. *I stress that both these processes are internal and have nothing to do with real relationships with external objects as the infant may understand them although brushes with the not yet understood outside world contributes to the generation of sensations within the infant.* The objects are created under pressure from libidinal and aggressive drives, through (internal) introjection and projection. This is in line with Melanie Klein's first theory of internal object-relations (see Mitchell [1981] on the development of Klein's theory of internal objects) where what is perceived as unpleasurable and bad is projected into a not-me bad object (created for this purpose) and what is pleasurable and therefore good is created into a not-me good object (each with corresponding self-representations). All of this is the ego's attempt to make sense out of new and conflictual affective experience. Affective experiences are split in two, good and bad, and only until the later depressive position do they consolidate into one good and bad whole object, and the self into a whole good and bad self. However, to my mind, these split object relations are only initially completely internally generated and transposed onto external object relations. Experiences with real objects help consolidate the goodness or badness of internal objects to the extent that the pleasurable sensation of milk in the baby's body, coming from the mother's breast, will aid in the generation of a good internal object and vice versa. I would agree with Winnicott that the object is first created but then is at some point found.

Why Object Protection?

This conception of internal objects generated to contain affective experience makes the idea of object protection, in the narcissistic defense, more plausible. The object is protected before the appearance of the external object in the registry of the child's psyche (before the child finds it) because it is the embodiment of the child's aggressive and libidinal impulses (and in a sense is the child's first creation). The aggressive drive forms its own sadistic internal object that may or may not find correspondence with externally generated frustrating and bad experiences. At the same time, the libidinal drive, in an effort to maintain a balance in the psyche, generates its own objects. The pleasurable affective states projected into the good internal object give it the life-sustaining and idealized qualities that make it into an indispensable good object without which the infant will die a painful and wretched death. Depending on the extent of the individual's narcissism, these internal objects are transposed in varying degrees onto real external objects. The object is then both feared and needed, and both are good enough reasons for the infant's psyche to avoid attacking it. Again, as detailed above, in my opinion the so-called destruction of the object which leads to the idea that "the object doesn't exist" is more accurately described as an ongoing attack on the psyche's ability to clearly and accurately perceive it. Thus what is meant by saying that the object is under a state of perpetual attack is, paradoxically, that the internal object is not harmed—rather it is "turned off" from one's perception. This I think is close to André Green's description of *zero object* (2001), *white* and *blank* psychosis (1999, 2001), and the process of de-objectalization (1999, 2001). *The object that is not there is still there-enough to provoke a defense.* Intrapsychically, ignorance is bliss. Like the moon to the earth, however, the object still exerts a pressure on the psyche that remains gravitational.

Mind and Object

It has been necessary for me to conceive of the early psyche as developing *in relation* to itself, in the sense of being occupied by events that make their impressions on the mind in ways that shape the individual's relationship to the world throughout his life. I prefer to use the *object* concept as one would view these mental events objectively, from the

292 □ R O D R I G O   B A R A H O N A

outside looking in, representing an experience with a thing that the infantile psyche does not yet understand to be inside or outside of itself, but that nevertheless occupies the space of an influencing *presence*. At the same time that the infant is aware of this presence, he does not yet understand that it is a part of himself (a projection of his own libidinal and aggressive impulses), but nevertheless undertakes the struggle to come to grips with it, a struggle that will remain at the center of his drive for life and death throughout all of development.

Conclusion

I hope that it is evident that what I am advocating is integration and open-mindedness, not eclecticism. The latter ignores the basic inconsistencies between theoretical assumptions underlying conflicting theories. A good example of this type of eclecticism, I think, is conveyed in Fred Pine's (1990) book on the four psychologies of psychoanalysis, where patients are viewed one moment through the lens of one model, the next from another, and so on, representing the moment-to-moment shifts in presentations of conflict in the patient. This type of eclecticism is what I was trying to avoid by elucidating some of the subtle discrepancies between basic Lacanian and modern discourse in the first part of this paper, only to advocate for the thoughtful integration of psychoanalytic disciplines in the latter part. Of course, Pine (1998) defends against charges of eclecticism by referring to his work as a "thoughtful integration of clinical ideas from various sources" (p. 47), which is exactly what I am proposing here.

Modern psychoanalysis, more than just being a theory of technique, *is* a theory of mind. Its theory is the theory of its students and practitioners who through phantasy, emotion, and intellectual understanding cannot accept that all along they have only been *doing* modern analysis without *thinking* about the psychic life of the patient in a certain modern analytic way. Modern psychoanalysis does not exist in and of itself, outside the mind of its practitioners and much less outside of the greater psychoanalytic community in general. It is created and it is found. Therefore, as we move further in modern psychoanalysis, throwing out and incorporating new and old theories and systems into our psychoanalytic *Weltanschauung*, let us not forget that as modern psychoanalysts we are, and have always been, Freudians, Kleinians, Winnicottians, Bionians, and Lacanians, as well as drive theorists and

relationists, modernists and post-modernists, and even hermeneuticists
—all the while that we were Spotnitzians and Meadovians—and thus in
the finest of psychoanalytic traditions, conflicted.

REFERENCES

Eagle, M. (1984), *Recent Developments in Psychoanalysis. A Critical Evaluation*. New York: McGraw-Hill.
Fink, B. (1997), *A Clinical Introduction to Lacanian Psychoanalysis: Theory and Technique*. Cambridge, MA: Harvard University Press.
Freud, S. (1911), Psychoanalytic notes on an autobiographical account of a case of paranoia. *Standard Edition*. London: Hogarth Press, 12: 9–82.
———— (1930), Civilization and its discontents. *Standard Edition*. London: Hogarth Press, 21:57–145.
Green, A. (1999), *The Work of the Negative*. London: Free Association Books.
———— (2001), *Life Narcissism, Death Narcissism*. London: Free Association Books.
Greenberg, J. R. & S. A. Mitchell (1983), *Object Relations in Psychoanalytic Theory*. Cambridge, MA: Harvard University Press.
Hurevitch, M. (1999), A commentary on Spotnitz's "The clinical pactice of modern psychoanalysis." *Modern Psychoanalysis*, 24:21–31.
Kirman, J. (1998), One-person or two-person psychology? *Modern Psychoanalysis*, 23:3–22.
Lacan, J. (1977), *Ecrits*. New York: W. W. Norton & Company.
Liegner, E. (1995), The anaclitic countertransference in resistance resolution. *Modern Psychoanalysis*, 20:153–164.
Marshall, R. (1998), Hyman Spotnitz and Heinz Kohut: contrasts and convergences. *Modern Psychoanalysis*, 23:183–196.
Meadow, P. W. (1999), Response to Hurevitch's discussion of Spotnitz's "The Clinical Practice of Modern Psychoanalysis." *Modern Psychoanalysis*, 24:33–36.
———— (1996a), Object relations in a drive theory model. *Modern Psychoanalysis*, 21:155–172.
———— (1996b), The myth of the impersonal analyst. *Modern Psychoanalysis*, 21:241–259.
———— (1996c), Selected theoretical and clinical papers. *Modern Psychoanalysis*, 21:129–380.

Mitchell, S. A. (1981), The origins and nature of the "object" in the theories of Klein and Fairbairn. *Contemporary Psychoanalysis*, 17:374–398.

Ogden, T. (1982), *Projective Identification and Psychotherapeutic Technique*. Northvale, NJ: Jason Aronson.

——— (1990), *The Matrix of the Mind: Object-relations and the Psychoanalytic Dialogue*. Northvale, NJ: Jason Aronson.

Pine, F. (1990), *Drive, Ego, Object, Self*. New York: Basic Books.

——— (1998), *Diversity and Direction in Psychoanalytic Technique*. New Haven, CT: Yale University Press.

Richards, A. D. (1999), A. A. Brill and the politics of exclusion. *Journal of the American Psychoanalytic Association*, 47:9–28.

Spotnitz, H. (1987), P*sychotherapy of Preoedipal Conditions*. Northvale, NJ: Jason Aronson.

——— (2004), *Modern Psychoanalysis of the Schizophrenic Patient*. 2004 Second Edition. New York: YBK Publishers.

Spotnitz, H. & P. W. Meadow (1995), *Treatment of the Narcissistic Neuroses*. Northvale, NJ: Jason Aronson.

Winnicott, D. W. (1965), *The Maturational Process and the Facilitating Environment*. New York: International Universities Press.

321 Summit Avenue #5
Brighton, MA 02135
rodrigo_barahona@bphc.org

Books Received

Anastasopoulos, Dimitris & Evangelos Papanicolaou. *The Therapist at Work: Personal Factors Affecting the Analytic Process.* New York: Karnac, 2004. 152 pp. paperback.

Bishop, Bernardine, Angela Foster, Josephine Klein & Victoria O'Connell, eds. *Elusive Elements in Practice.* London: Karnac, 2004. 99 pp. paperback.

Caplan, Paula J. & Lisa Cosgrove, eds. *Bias in Psychiatric Diagnosis.* Lanham, MD: Jason Aronson, 2004. 269 pp. softcover.

Casement, Ann, ed. *Who Owns Psychoanalysis?* New York: Karnac, 2004. 396 pp. paperback.

Davoine, Francoise & Jean-Max Gaudilliere. *History beyond Trauma.* Susan Fairfield, translator. New York: Other Press, 2004. 282 pp. paperback.

Eigen, Michael. *The Sensitive Self.* Middletown, CT: Wesleyan University Press, 2004. 196 pp. paperback

Faber, M. D. *The Psychological Roots of Religious Belief: Searching for Angels and the Parent-God.* Amherst, NY: Prometheus Books, 2004. 245 pp.

Flores, Philip J. *Addiction as an Attachment Disorder.* Lanham, MD: Rowman & Littlefield, 2004. 272 pp.

Goldberg, Arnold. *Misunderstanding Freud.* New York: Other Press, 2004. 233 pp.

Goldstein, William N. & Samuel T. Goldberg. *Using the Transference in Psychotherapy.* Lanham, MD: Rowman & Littlefield, 2004. 153 pp.

Gould, Laurence J., Lionel F. Stapley & Mark Stein, eds. *Experiential Learning in Organizations: Applications of the Tavistock Group Relations Approach.* London: Karnac, 2004. 192 pp. paperback.

Harari, Roberto. *Lacan's Four Fundamental Concepts of Psychoanalysis: An Introduction*. Judith Filc, translator. New York: Other Press, 2004. 296 pp. paperback

King, Robert A., Peter B. Neubauer, Samuel Abrams & A. Scott Dowling. *The Psychoanalytic Studies of the Child*. Vol. 58. New Haven, CT: Yale University Press, 2003. 331 pp.

Laine, Aira, ed. *Power of Understanding: Essays in Honour of Veikko Tahka*. New York: London, 2004. 335 pp. paperback.

Maguire, Anne. *Skin Disease: A Message from the Soul—A Treatise from a Jungian Perspective of Psychosomatic Dermatology*. London: Free Association Books, 2004. 206 pp. paperback.

McWilliams, Nancy. *Psychoanalytic Pyschotherapy: A Practicioner's Guide*. New York: The Guilford Press, 2004. 353 pp.

Micale, Mark S., ed. *The Mind of Modernism: Medicine, Psychology, and the Cultureal Arts in Europe and America, 1880–1940*. Palo Alto, CA: Stanford University Press, 2003. 455 pp. paperback.

Pearson, Jenny, ed. *Analyst of the Imagination: The Life and Work of Charles Rycroft*. New York: Karnac, 2004. 258 pp. paperback.

Rachman, Arnold W. *Psychotherapy of Difficult Cases*. Madison, CT: Psychosocial Press, 2003. 351 pp. paperback.

Ragland, Ellie & Dragan Milovanovick, eds. *Lacan: Topologically Speaking*. New York: Other Press, 2004. 397 pp. paperback.

Rank, Otto. *The Myth of the Birth of the Hero: A Psychological Exploration of Myth*. Gregory C. Richter & E. James Lieberman, translators. Baltimore: The Johns Hopkins University Press, 2004. 149 pp.

Reeder, Jurgen. *Hate and Love in Psychoanalytic Insitutions: The Dilemma of a Profession*. New York: Other Press, 2004. 310 pp. paperback.

Roazen, Paul. *On the Freud Watch: Public Memoirs*. London: Free Association Books, 2003. 224 pp. paperback.

Schlesinger, Herbert J. *The Texture of Treatment: On the Matter of Psychoanalytic Technique*. Hillsdale, NJ: The Analytic Press, 2003. 292 pp.

Socarides, Charles W. & Loretta R. Loeb, eds. *The Mind of the Paedophile: Psychoanalytic Perspectives*. London: Karnac Books, 2004. 211 pp. paperback

Tessman, Lora Heims. *The Analyst's Analyst Within*. Hillsdale, NJ: The Analytic Press, 2003. 292 pp.

About the Authors

BARAHONA, RODRIGO, M.A., is in private practice in Brookline, MA. He is also a psychotherapist with the outpatient unit at Arbour Hospital and the substance abuse unit of the Boston Public Health Commission. He is an advanced psychoanalytic candidate at the Boston Graduate School of Psychoanalysis Certificate Program and is finalizing his doctorate studies at the Cyril Z. Meadow Institute of Psychoanalysis in Vermont.

BIGDA-PEYTON, FRANCES, Ed.D, is on the faculty of the Institute for the Study of Violence and serves as field work coordinator for that program. She frequently lectures on innovative approaches to couples therapy. She is in private practice in Brookline, MA.

KIRMAN, NICOLE, Ph.D., is a certified psychoanalyst in private practice in New York City. She is a faculty member, training analyst, and supervisor at the Center for Modern Psychoanalytic Studies. She is the author of "The Repetition Compulsion Revisited."

MACKAY, NIGEL, Ph.D., is a senior lecturer in psychology at the University of Wollongong, New South Wales, Australia. He is author of the monograph *Motivation and Explanation: An Essay on Freud's Philosophy of Psychology* and numerous articles on philosophical and methodological issues in psychology and psychoanalysis.

MCALOON, ROSE FICHERA, Ph.D., is a faculty member of the Center for Modern Psychoanalytic Studies and director of its extension

© 2004 CMPS/*Modern Psychoanalysis*, Vol. 29, No. 2

division. She is also the director of the Italian American Psychotherapy Center and serves as the vice president of the Pirandello Society of America. She writes and lectures on various topics including psychoanalysis and literature. Her private practice is in Manhattan and includes group and individual work with doctoral candidates struggling to complete dissertations.

POSER, STEVEN, Ph.D., is coordinator of the research committee and training analyst at the Center for Modern Psychoanalytic Studies. An exhibiting painter, he received the 1997 NAAP Gradiva award for visual art. He is in private practice in New York City and Salt Point, NY.

SEMEL, VICKI G., Ph.D., is executive director of the Academy of Clinical and Applied Psychoanalysis in West Orange, NJ and director of admissions at the Center for Modern Psychoanalytic Studies, and a training and supervisory analyst at both schools. Among her published works is *Strategies for Treatment with the Elderly: Living with Hope and Meaning*, Second Edition, which is forthcoming.

SHEPHERD, MARY, M.A., is a training and supervising analyst and an associate professor at the Boston Graduate School of Psychoanalysis where she is also the public information officer. She has written on modern psychoanalytic history and anaclitic countertransference considerations. Her current research interest involves the attempt to integrate aspects of psychoanalytic meta-theory with the recent discoveries of neuroscience.

Printed in the United States
37686LVS00006BA/1-213

9 780976 435945